John
Always be prudent —
Guerdon

Uncertainty is a Certainty:

Fables for Fiduciaries

Guerdon T. Ely
MBA, CFP®, AIFA®

Foreword by W. Scott Simon, author of *The Prudent Investor Act: A Guide to Understanding*

Ely Prudent Portfolios, LLC
Chico, California

xulon PRESS

Uncertainty is a Certainty
Fables for Fiduciaries (And You May Be One)
by Guerdon T. Ely, MBA, CFP,® AIFA®

Printed in the United States of America

ISBN 9781615795970

**Some names and locations have been changed to protect the innocent (or guilty), but all anecdotal stories are true and based on author's personal experiences.*

Requests for permission or further information should be addressed to Ely Prudent Portfolios, LLC, gtely@elyportfolios.com.

gtely@elyportfolios.com
http://www.elyportfolios.com

www.xulonpress.com

Dedication

I would like to dedicate this book to my three daughters, who believe their dad can do anything, and to my wife who believes it too, even though she should know better.

Foreword

It's my feeling that Guerdon Ely asked me to write the foreword to this book, *Uncertainty is a Certainty: Fables for Fiduciaries*, for two reasons. First, I'm a friend and colleague of his, and second, one of the books that I have written is *The Prudent Investor Act: A Guide to Understanding*. My book, coming in at just over 135,000 words, including (count 'em) 997 footnotes, is a tome on modern prudent fiduciary investing. "Modern" prudent fiduciary investing began with publication of the Restatement (Third) of Trusts (Prudent Investor Rule) in 1992 and the Uniform Prudent Investor Act in 1994, and has continued since then with a large outpouring of legal model acts progeny. I have also been writing a monthly column for Morningstar called "Fiduciary Focus" since 2003. I figure that I've written over one-quarter million words for that column through the years, not to mention all the words in other articles that I have authored and co-authored.

All of this is to set the context for why I am so peeved at Guerdon. He has managed to convey in a few thousand words the meaning of modern prudent fiduciary investing in a way that I never could in hundreds of thousands of words. I cannot be sure, but as far as I know I'm the only person to have read my own book cover to cover and I don't mind telling you that even for me it was a real struggle. Guerdon's book, in contrast, is accessible to the average reader as well as to fiduciaries of all stripes - whether professional or amateur – as a book that they will actually *want* to read because it is highly informative and funny too. I'm sure that any fiduciary would rather learn about the ins and outs of modern prudent fiduciary investing with a smile on their face – and even the occasional outright belly-laugh – than to set out and endure the Death March of reading my writings on this vitally important subject.

Guerdon's book couldn't be more user-friendly as he takes you through all the major issues of modern prudent fiduciary investing. These include understanding what a trust document is, the meaning of Modern Portfolio Theory, the usefulness of an investment policy statement and the importance of following a prudent investment process. In addition, he covers the duty of care, the duty of skill, the duty of caution, the duty to invest in a portfolio context, the duty to determine the risk tolerance of a trust, the duty to ascertain the investment time horizon of a trust, the duty to manage and monitor investments and any investment agents retained, the duty to investigate, the fundamental duty to trade off risk and return in trust portfolios and a myriad of other duties. Guerdon always discusses these important duties with a humorous bent that helps contribute so much to actually understanding them.

I enthusiastically recommend Guerdon's fine book to you and I am sure that you will thoroughly enjoy reading it as it deepens your understanding of modern prudent fiduciary investing. Heck, even if you have no interest at all in modern prudent fiduciary investing you will like this book. For example, Guerdon tells you – because he held a job where he actually did it - not only how to weigh honey bees but also how to place them in a package ready for shipping. No book on modern prudent fiduciary investing, that I know of, lets you in on that kind of information.

W. Scott Simon
Principal
Prudent Investor Advisors, LLC
October 27, 2009

Acknowledgements

"Nuts! I didn't get it." was the PG-rated version of what Jim Kelly heard in his earpiece as he was describing the action at the Tradition Golf Tournament. I was in a trailer helping with TV graphics and could hear the producer's profanity-laced comments in my own earpiece, while at the same time hearing the live feed of announcers through a speaker. The producer had promised Kelly that he would get the hole number Jack Nicklaus was on but, as his statement indicated, he didn't get it. What amazed me was that Kelly had already started his sentence by the time Nicklaus' image appeared on the screen but his voice gave no indication of the dilemma. Kelly smoothly substituted "he's on the back nine" in place of the missing hole number. Golf telecasts look so effortless and peaceful but what you don't see are the dozens of staffer's frantically working behind the scenes gathering, coordinating, and arranging pictures, sound, and content into an informative and enjoyable program. As my story illustrates, there is a reason why they call the announcers "talent," but the talent of the announcers alone could never create a golf telecast.

I've found out that writing a book isn't much different. It takes far more than just an author to create a book. There are so many people that helped with this book that I cannot name them all and the ones I do name, I could never thank enough.

I especially want to thank my assistant Deborah Cockrell who spent hours checking my spelling, punctuation, and grammar, in addition to editing and organizing my rambling thoughts.

I also want to thank my technical advisor Ken Noble who, in addition to creating the most incredibly efficient investment advisory office, has been gracious enough to proofread and critique my book on his own time.

One of my biggest supporters has been my daughter Anna, but that support has not gotten in the way of her objectivity. I can always count on Anna for an accurate and honest opinion, even when I don't want to hear it.

Without the help of Michael Nevens, John Pattison, and Steven Yarbrough, this book wouldn't even have been an idea, let alone a reality. Just like I know the steps that make up a prudent investment process, Michael, John and Steven know the steps necessary to professionally create, edit and market a book.

Finally I'd like to thank those individuals who reviewed and commented on drafts of the book. Included in that list are Ed Knight, Carolynn Reynolds, George Coughlin, David O'Leary, Marion O'Leary, Glenn Freed, Katherine Simmonds and Scott Simon. I would also like to thank my sister Charlotte, my daughters Hillary and Sarah, and my wife Barbara.

About the Author

Many people have difficulty spelling the author's name, but 13-year-old Sameer Mishra got it right: "g-u-e-r-d-o-n." Guerdon means "financial reward" and it was the winning word at the 2008 Scripps National Spelling Bee.

Guerdon Ely, MBA, CFP®, AIFA® has over 25 years of experience in financial and investment counseling. He is the creator and developer of two highly regarded retirement distribution software programs, MRD-Determinator and Pre-Determinator, which have been reviewed in MorningstarAdvisor.Com, Investment Advisor, Accounting Today, and WebCPA. He also is the founder of Ely Prudent Portfolios, LLC, an investment advisory firm.

Mr. Ely received a Master of Business Administration degree from California State University, Chico after graduating from the University of California at Santa Barbara with a degree in Economics. He is a Certified Financial Planner™, an Accredited Investment Fiduciary Analyst™, and a Chartered Financial Consultant®.

Mr. Ely has taught courses for the California Continuing Education of the Bar and other professional organizations. He has contributed to educational materials used at American Law Institute-American Bar Association programs, at the Notre Dame Tax Institute, and the Heckerling Institute on Estate Planning. His contributions on various financial subjects have appeared in articles in Newsweek, Forbes, Bloomberg, Trusts and Estates, Retirement Weekly, and The Wall Street Journal.

Mr. Ely has also been acknowledged for his contributions to *The Prudent Investor Act: A Guide to Understanding* by W. Scott Simon, *Life and Death Planning for Retirement Benefits* by Natalie Choate and *The Terrible Truth About Investing* by Bruce J. Temkin.

If you would like to discuss things related to the contents of this book or schedule Mr. Ely as a speaker or consultant for your estate, organization or conference, please call 1-800-560-0636 or visit his website at http://www.elyportfolios.com/contactus.

Preface

"I see what you are saying by what you do," said my fifth-grade Sunday school teacher, Mrs. Revenaugh. I was relieved that someone finally "got it." Being incredibly shy I was afraid to talk with people so I tried to show them what I believed by what I did.

Actions have always meant more to me than words. To me, actions start with attitude. There is no shortage of people who can (and will) tell you what you should do but there are very few who are willing to consistently do what they think is right, no matter what it costs them. People like this seem to define success in life, not by how much they can get, but by how much they can give. Included in this book are stories of such people, my heroes.

About now, you are probably confused because you thought this was a manual for fiduciaries. Have no fear, it is, but the stories of my heroes have been incorporated because it is my hope that their selfless attitudes and actions will inspire fiduciaries who are reading this book. I truly believe that fiduciaries cannot fulfill their legal obligations without also accepting a moral obligation to serve the beneficiaries of the trusts, charities, or pensions whose investments they are responsible for managing. This being said, it is important to note that fiduciaries are not judged on good intentions, or even on good results, but solely on their actions. The law requires fiduciaries to follow an objectively defined set of duties and responsibilities that are known as a "prudent process."

The reason why fiduciaries are judged exclusively on their adherence to a prudent process is because, even with the best intentions and the best planning, an investment strategy can fail. In this uncertain world, markets do not always reward prudent decisions, even by the most experienced and best-trained investors. Michael Jordan once said, "Twenty-six times I've been trusted to take the game winning shot and missed... I can accept failure, everyone fails at something. But I can't accept not trying."[1] Likewise, fiduciaries are not held responsible for failures but they *are* held responsible for not following a prudent process, the legal version of "not trying."

In that sense fiduciaries do not need to fear uncertainty because they are not legally responsible for results as long as they follow a prudent process. But, a good fiduciary is concerned with more than just personal legal liability. The well-being of his or her beneficiary should be the highest concern. This is where life humbles us all; we can put the interests of our trust, pension, or charitable beneficiaries first and we can do the right things, but we can never be certain of the results.

I always thought that I wasn't that good of an investment advisor because I didn't have all the answers — now I know that no one does. In life, uncertainty is a certainty. So, as a fiduciary, worry about the things you can control and not about the things you can't. The law gets it and I hope you do too; as a fiduciary you are being judged, not on results but, by the words of my Sunday school teacher, "I see what you are saying by what you do."

Table of Contents

Introduction

"It's time to get ready for bed." Those were words of both dread and excitement for me as a young boy. I didn't want to go to bed, but I *did* want my mother to read me a bedtime story. My favorites were *Aesop Fables*: *The Hare and the Tortoise, The Boy Who Cried Wolf, The Ant and The Grasshopper, The Wolf in Sheep's Clothing,* and so on. It's been almost half a century since she last read me those stories, but I still remember each tale and the underlying moral. "Slow and steady wins the race." "No one will believe a liar, even when he is telling the truth." "Save in the good time to prepare for the hard times." And, "Appearances can be deceiving."

To me, stories have always been the best way to communicate ideas. That is why this book has been written as a series of amusing and thought-provoking anecdotes designed to help fiduciaries visualize, understand, and remember the often complicated and confusing requirements of their position. I like to think of it as *Fables for Fiduciaries*.

Purpose

Obviously, this is a book for fiduciaries, but just who is a fiduciary? Simply put, a fiduciary is anyone responsible for managing someone else's money. But how do they do that? What are they supposed to do? Are they legally bound to behave in certain ways and follow certain procedures? What differentiates a good fiduciary from the bad and the ugly ones? The purpose of this book is to accurately answer these questions in an enjoyable and entertaining manner. Equipped with these answers, fiduciaries will be better able to fulfill their duties to the individuals or entities whose money they are managing, and in the process limit their personal financial liability. Since it is written at a level which laymen should be able to comprehend, it is hoped that attorneys, CPAs, pension administrators, and other professionals who advise clients who are fiduciaries, will give copies of this book to those clients.

The Uniform Prudent Investor Act

The Uniform Prudent Investor Act ("UPIA", "Act") "... regulates the investment responsibilities of trustees" of private trusts. While its terms apply to trusts, its standards are "...expected to inform the investment responsibilities of directors and officers of charitable corporations." Its principles are even "...applicable to [pension] fiduciaries." Therefore, this book uses the Uniform Prudent Investor Act as the main guide, with reference to other laws, for defining the standards of prudent fiduciary investing. It is my belief that all fiduciaries should understand the Uniform Prudent Investor Act because its standards form the basis of the interpretation of prudence for fiduciaries regulated by that Act and by other fiduciary laws.

The Book Sections

The book is organized into eight sections. The first examines what you need to know. The second is about where to go to get what you need to know. The third shows the consequences of knowing but not doing. The fourth explores the duties of a fiduciary, which require action as well as knowledge. The fifth is on knowing what works and what doesn't. The sixth address the battle between knowledge and emotions. The seventh is about my heroes who know what really is important in life. And the eighth is a reminder that the standards of prudent fiduciary investing are objective and, therefore, knowable.

Limitations

The book touches on most, if not all, of the duties, responsibilities, and requirements of the Uniform Prudent Investor Act, both stated and implied. However, the book is not intended to be used as a tool for the *legal* interpretation of the Act.

About the Writing Style

I am a fiduciary and I take my duties very seriously, but I refuse to take myself too seriously. You may be a fiduciary too. Hopefully my stories and self-deprecating humor will keep you entertained, but, more important, I hope they will help you understand and remember your legal and moral responsibilities as a fiduciary. So, if these fables make you chuckle — that's good; if they make you think — that's better; and if they inspire you to do better — that's the best.

Section 1

Need to Know: What is a Fiduciary, Who is a Fiduciary, and What is expected of a Fiduciary?

"If you don't know where you're going, any direction will get you there."
- Lou Gerstner, IBM

"Know thyself" is an ancient Greek saying, and it's not bad advice for a fiduciary.
Knowing what you are as a fiduciary and what is expected of you gives purpose and direction to your role as a fiduciary.

What is a Fiduciary?

You know how a term becomes so familiar that you just assume it is so for everyone? Sort of like the authors of manuals for TV remote controls: the instructions may make sense to the writers, but to rest of us the directions are completely undecipherable. So it appears to be with the word "fiduciary." When I wrote the first draft of this book, I just assumed that the word was so familiar it didn't need to be defined. However, I quickly found out that wasn't the case. Even a local judge gave me a rambling answer that left both his wife and me saying, "Huh?" As a matter of fact, the most common response I got when I asked people, "What is a fiduciary?" was a bewildered pause, followed by them breaking out in song with the line "Fidelity Fiduciary Bank," from the 1964 Disney film, *Mary Poppins*.

When I hear that line, I think of another bank, the Waukesha County Marine Bank. It was my grandfather's bank and I think his story is an appropriate and effective way for me to define, "What is a Fiduciary?"

My father was Joseph B. Ely, Jr. and so his dad was Joseph, Sr., but we called him JoJo instead of calling him Grandpa Joe. JoJo started his own bank in the "go-go" years of the early twentieth century when there was an explosion of banks, especially very small banks. According to John R. Walter in his article *Depression-Era Bank Failures: The Great*

Contagion or the Great Shakeout?, many of "...these new small banks were formed in small towns and rural communities — especially in the corn and cotton belts of the country... [where] rising prices of farm commodities along with rising farm real estate values may have played a significant role in the attractiveness of rural banking..." Whatever the reason, JoJo started his bank in a small Midwestern town during this time. However, as Walter points out "...too many [of these] banks were formed without adequate financial or managerial resources..." and the rapid growth in numbers caused the banking market to be "overbanked." This excess banking capacity, along with a downturn in farming prices, caused more than half of these small Midwestern banks to fail between 1921 and 1930, and the onset of the Great Depression only accelerated this rate of failure.

In this bleak environment my grandfather proved his character. My dad's bedroom was above his parent's, and through the un-insulated floor he could hear his mother's sobs and his father's less than confident attempts to reassure her that everything would be all right. Every night, my dad would hear his mom crying and his father discussing the bleakness of their situation. But every morning he would watch his father put on his suit, walk to the bank, sit on his wooden stool and face his fears. Day after day he paid out bank assets until they were all gone, and then he started paying out his own. He sold his house and his farm and used that cash to cover the run on his bank, because he believed it was his duty to his depositors.

A fiduciary is someone who accepts the responsibility of taking care of the property of another person or entity. And, according to the summary of the Uniform Management of Public Employee Retirement Systems, the level of responsibility is "...the highest standard of conduct in the management of investment assets...that the law can establish...[and it] carries the greatest burden of care, loyalty, and utmost good faith..." I'm not sure JoJo could have correctly answered, "What is a fiduciary?" but you could have learned what a fiduciary is by watching him. When he accepted the responsibility for his depositors' accounts, and when he put their financial interests above his own, he showed his depositors, his family, and his community the answer to the question, "What is a fiduciary?"

You May Be a Fiduciary if You are Responsible For Managing Someone Else's Money

"Am I your father or are you mine?" I was aware that my father was becoming more dependent on me, but I never realized the extent of the role reversal until he uttered that question. Dad was ninety-five and the combination of age and pain medications had dimmed a once bright mind. Although he never seemed to lose his incredible sense of logic, the confusing inputs his brain was receiving made for illogical and, sometimes, humorous outputs. His brain was always active, but you never knew if the impulse causing it to fire was an actual event or an illusionary one.

I remember one night he went on a 2:00 a.m. rampage in his rest home, going from door to door rousting the residents to go fight an imaginary forest fire. The rest home called to notify me that the paramedics had taken Dad to the hospital. I arrived at the emergency room just as the doctor was beginning his examination. When the doctor asked Dad if he knew where he was, Dad said, "I'm in a boxcar." The doctor informed him that he was actually in a hospital and then asked, "Do you know who I am?" Dad looked at him and made no response. So the doctor asked again, "Look at what I am wearing. Do you know who I am?" Dad looked at him and then turned to the nurse with a funny grin and said, "You'd better get me another doctor, this guy doesn't know who he is."

Dad was always in charge. It wasn't "his way or the highway," it was just "his way." And his way was rigid structure supported by his phenomenal organizational skills. That's why he was put in charge of most all the big fires in the Western United States when he was a US Forest Service fire control officer. He could instantly organize hundreds of firefighters, dozens of fire trucks, bulldozers and other pieces of equipment, and numerous fire retardant dropping airplanes into a coordinated and effective firefighting team. After helping Dad with a tax issue, my CPA remarked, "Your dad is so organized that he makes Fred look sloppy." And Fred was a guy in town who was legendary for his time-management practices. It was suspected that even Fred's potty-stops were pre-scheduled in his day-timer. Knowing this, you can imagine the surprise my sister and I experienced when Dad told his attorney, "Yes, I want Guerdon to have total control of all my finances." And then he signed the paperwork resigning as trustee of his trust and making me the sole trustee of all his assets.

According to the Center for Fiduciary Studies (also known as fi360™,) "the vast majority of the nation's liquid investible wealth is in the hands of investment fiduciaries..." Most of this wealth is held in family trusts (like my dad's), pensions, and charitable foundations. There is a very good chance that if you aren't a fiduciary now, you will be at some time in your life. As a trustee of my father's family trust, I was responsible for managing his money when he was no longer capable. Since the funds in the trust ultimately were distributed to me and my siblings, I was a fiduciary accountable not only to my father, but also to my brother and sisters. For the past twelve years I have been on the board of a local charity, and since that charity has an endowment fund, I am also a fiduciary for that fund and am answerable to my state's Attorney General. In addition, as the owner of a business with a retirement plan, I am a fiduciary to the participants and beneficiaries of that plan, which is monitored by the Department of Labor. And finally, as a Registered Investment Advisor, I am a fiduciary to my clients, with my activities regulated by the Securities and Exchange Commission.

You can see from my situation that it is not unusual to be a fiduciary. However, it has been my experience that most people are not aware of what a fiduciary is and most fiduciaries aren't even aware that they are one. As fi360 notes, "It is not uncommon for fiduciaries to be unaware of their status." So, how do you know if you are a fiduciary? To paraphrase Jeff Foxworthy, "You may be a..." fiduciary if you are responsible for managing someone else's money.

It's the Process, Stupid!

"I hate you! I hate you! I hate you!" Sammy* yelled as he rushed down the aisle and attacked the poster of Smokey Bear. Before continuing, I must tell you (in the interest of full disclosure) that he didn't actually use the words, "I hate," but I changed the expletive in the interest of decency. Sammy, who looked amazingly like a miniature Fatty Arbuckle, was a ward of the court placed in the care of the Canyon Boys Ranch*, a facility for juvenile delinquent and seriously emotionally disturbed teenage boys. Since the ranch was located in the middle of the woods, a forest ranger had been in the dining hall giving the boys a talk on fire safety. When he pointed at Smokey Bear's picture on his easel and said, "Now, Smokey doesn't like little boys who play with matches," it was like he lit a match under our resident pyromaniac.

Sammy and the other boys were likeable enough kids who were difficult to like because either bad genes or bad environments had stunted their ability to interact appropriately with other people. The same probably could be said for the work staff. At a salary of a dollar a day, plus room and board, the only people the job tended to attract were those who liked the remote location because *they* were trying to hide from something: a spouse, the law, or reality. We were a very dysfunctional hippie version of *Friends*,[2] but we were idealistic enough to believe that, with good nutrition, physical activity, and lots of one-on-one time, we could do a better job of rehabilitating these kids than the typical "lock 'em up and drug 'em up" factory.

The boys were all juvenile delinquents who, because of crimes or the inability of their parents to control them, became wards of the court. The Ranch was appointed as their legal guardian, our boss ran the operation, we were the counselors, and the whole thing was supervised by two psychiatrists, Joe and Cybil* — a husband and wife version of Laurel and Hardy in both appearance and actions. They preached "no drugs, good food, and exercise" while they consumed more drugs than Keith Richards, more hamburgers than Ronald McDonald®, and more time on their butts than Norm on his *Cheers* barstool.[3]

Guardians can be responsible for either person or property, or both. In our case, we were guardians of the person, not the property. We were responsible for raising someone else's kids. It was our job to take care of their physical needs, educate them, and instill moral values. We were, in effect, substitute parents. If we had also been guardians of the property, we would have been fiduciaries, substitute financial decision makers.

At the ranch we had a policy and procedure manual for the counselors. The policies were a guide for decision making and the procedures were a series of steps (an established order) designed to facilitate the accomplishment of the policies. For fiduciaries, the overriding "policy" is prudence and the "procedures" are the processes for accomplishing prudent decision making. The Uniform Prudent Investor Act and other fiduciary laws are, therefore, the "policy and procedure manuals" for fiduciaries. They describe the duties fiduciaries must follow to ensure that a prudent process is established for the management and investment of financial assets.

The decisions we made as counselors changed with the circumstance of the situation, but the process never changed because the process was designed to put the best interests of the child first. "Accordingly, the portfolio decisions resulting from application of the prudence standard differ from case to case. However, the broad outline of a fiduciary's duty of prudent investing should be the same regardless of whether [the fiduciary] is a director of a foundation, a college or pension fund trustee, or the trustee of a private trust."[4] To put it in words Sammy would use, "It's the process, stupid!"

**Names have been changed*

Section 2

Getting Information: Understanding Trusts, Modern Portfolio Theory, Investment Policy Statements, and a Prudent Process

"Know where to find the information and how to use it. That is the secret of success"
- Albert Einstein

As a fiduciary, you need to know where to go to get information. First, you need to look at the trust or other controlling document for instructions. To properly manage the investment portfolio, you need a basic understanding of economics. An investment policy statement is needed to keep you on track. And finally, all these elements are tied together in a prudent process, which is the set of rules you must follow.

A Trust is for the Beneficiaries and a Refuge is for the Birds

When I was in college I worked a summer job at the Sacramento National Wildlife Refuge (SNWR), just south of the little farm town of Willows, CA. Each year, millions of migratory birds travel the Pacific Flyway and more than half of them use the SNWR as a feeding and rest stop. In the fall, there are so many birds it looks like a scene from Alfred Hitchcock's *The Birds*[5] which, according to my coworkers, it was. They claim that in 1962 they helped a "Hollywood" film crew shoot scenes of thousands of excited birds by setting off duck bombs in fields full of ducks and geese. I was never able to verify their claim, so it may have been a "rural legend." (Our town wasn't large enough to qualify for urban legends.)

Working at the refuge was a great summer job. I did all kinds of odd jobs, but my biggest tasks were replacing fencing and putting in sign posts. Over a couple of summers we replaced about 20 miles of fencing. My best guess is that I personally installed 5,000 metal t-posts, 250 wooden fence posts, and 200 sign posts. However, those numbers could be wrong. As the t-shirt I received from my kids keeps reminding me, "The older I get the better I was."

The fence I worked on circled the outer edge of the refuge. Inside this perimeter we grew rice and maintained wetlands for the benefit of migratory birds and other animals that used the refuge. This was consistent with the mission of the Wildlife Service which is "...to conserve, protect, and enhance fish, wildlife, plants, and their habitats." To fulfill this mission, the Wildlife Service acquires refuge land under legislative laws, executive orders, or other means. The purpose of each refuge is determined based upon "... the law, proclamation, executive order, agreement, public land order, donation document, or administrative memorandum establishing, authorizing, or expanding a refuge..." For example, the SNWR was created by Executive Order in 1937 with the stated purpose that it was to be used "...as a refuge and breeding ground for migratory birds and other wildlife."

A refuge is very similar to a trust. According *to Black's Law Dictionary*, a trust "...is a property interest held by one person (the trustee) at the request of another (the settlor) for the benefit of a third party (the beneficiary)."[6] In the SNWR's case, the property is held by the Wildlife Service at the request of the President for the benefit of the birds. Just as the executive order set out the purpose of the refuge and the conditions under which it was to be managed, so does a trust document describe the purposes and conditions under which trust assets are to be managed. The settlor (creator) of a trust has the freedom to set the rules for how the trust assets are to be managed and who the assets are going to benefit. The duty of the trustee is similar to the duty of the refuge manager in that they are both responsible for making sure the creator's wishes, as set forth in the trust document, are carried out in the best interests of the beneficiaries. Where the gift documents are silent or vague, the refuge manager relies on the Wildlife Service's regulations and the trustee relies on the Uniform Prudent Investor Act ("Act").

If the trust document is in conflict with the Uniform Prudent Investor Act, the trust trumps the Act because, as the Act notes, its requirements are default rules — that is, "rules that the settlor may alter or abrogate." The situation is similar for fiduciaries of charities but not for pension plans, since the minimum standards of the Employee Retirement Income Security Act (ERISA) cannot be altered. Nevertheless, fiduciaries of private trusts, charities, and pension plans all need to be familiar with both the controlling documents as well as the applicable laws in order to prudently perform their duties. Like the wildlife refuge manager, fiduciaries need to know the conditions and follow the rules if the purpose of the trust, charity, pension (or refuge) is going to be realized for the beneficiary, donee, employee, (or bird).

Modern Portfolio Theory is the Economic Foundation for Prudent Investing

Pounding nails into steel would have been easier than trying to drive them into hundred-year-old hemlock studs. I was remodeling old Victorian homes in Toronto, and that meant replacing the lath and plaster walls with sheetrock. Back in the 1970s, we didn't have screw guns, so we hung the sheetrock with ribbed sheetrock nails. In the battle between the sharp nail and the hard wood it was usually my arm that was the casualty. My boss, who had been doing this for years, would tap the nail into the sheetrock and then drive it home with two mighty blows. He would get a steady rhythm going like a good drummer; tap-bang-bang, tap-bang-bang, tap-bang-bang. I, on the other hand, was like Steve Martin in *The Jerk*[7] with absolutely no rhythm; each tap would be followed by numerous and uneven bangs punctuated with my favorite expletive. With all this inefficient, extra motion it didn't take long to completely exhaust myself, forcing a switch to a two-handed forehand swing for nailing walls and to a two-handed backhand motion for the ceiling. To me, restoring Victorians was more like an episode of *Survivor*[8] than it was *Extreme Makeover: Home Edition.*[9]

Old Victorians may be beautiful, but they aren't too practical with their small rooms, wandering hallways, and cramped kitchens and bathrooms. To modernize them, you need to remove walls and open up spaces, which is challenging because most of the walls are load-bearing. In addition, the windows need replacing, the wiring must be upgraded, the walls have to be insulated, and the whole thing needs painting. The finished product is more open, lighter, more energy efficient, and more functional. A good remodel requires not only modern building materials and fixtures but, above all, careful planning.

Just as building practices have changed over time, the investment practices of fiduciaries have also experienced significant change. According to the Prefatory Note, "The Uniform Prudent Investor Act undertakes to update trust investment law in recognition of the alterations that have occurred in investment practice. These changes have occurred under the influence of a large and broadly accepted body of empirical and theoretical knowledge about the behavior of capital markets, often described as Modern Portfolio Theory."

Modern Portfolio Theory assumes that investors are rational and risk-averse, and that markets are efficient at pricing stocks. Therefore, when making a choice among investments with the same expected return, a rational investor would choose the one with the least risk. To take on increased risk, a rational investor would need to be compensated by higher expected returns. To accept lower expected returns, a rational investor would require a corresponding reduction in risk. Since, according to the theory, concentration in a limited number of stocks is not rewarded with higher expected returns, rational investors will always diversify their portfolios. To reduce risk as much as possible, a rational investor diversifies across companies, industries, business sectors, and countries. When codifying Modern

Portfolio Theory into the Act, the drafters of the Uniform Prudent Investor Act basically replaced the economic term "rational" with the legal term "prudent."

When we were remodeling old Victorian homes, we modernized them and brought them into conformity with modern building codes. Similarly, trustees and other fiduciaries need to bring their investment and management practices into conformity with the new "building codes" of the Uniform Prudent Investor Act. Modern Portfolio Theory is the economic foundation on which these modern prudent fiduciary codes are built.

An Investment Policy Statement is The Landmark That Keeps You on Track

The appearance of the jet, the vibration of its turbulence, and the roar of its engines were all simultaneous — like a lightning strike that is so close there is no delay between the flash of light and the crash of thunder. I was on a tractor disking fields along the western foothills of Northern California, and this wasn't the first time that an Air National Guard pilot had buzzed me. They routinely used the sparsely populated area along the foothills to do their low altitude flight training, and I think they routinely enjoyed scaring the crap out of me. A T-33 trainer jet is not a particularly big or fast jet, but when it's going 450 miles per hour only 150 feet above your head it definitely gets your attention.

The tractor I was operating was a Caterpillar Diesel 65 crawler. A crawler tractor is basically a bulldozer without a blade. We used crawler tractors before the introduction of big four wheel drive tractors, because only a crawler had enough power to pull a big disk through hard ground. The Cat was incredibly noisy and its high-pitched squeak is probably the reason why farmers my age are all deaf to high-pitched sounds. But as loud as the darn thing was, the clatter of the tracks was so rhythmic, it actually lulled me to sleep.

Besides being loud, the beast was incredibly hot. There was no insulation or even any sheet metal between me and the engine. I just sat there in the 100 degree valley heat with 350 degree exhaust manifolds just a few feet away. To keep from frying, I had a five-gallon bucket of water and an old rag. I would dip the rag in the water and put it under my cowboy hat. With the dust kicked up by the disks, the water would turn to mud by the end of the day. It was hot as hell, noisy as hell, dirty as hell, and fun as hell. I was outside all day and I got to drive this big old piece of equipment when I wasn't even old enough to drive a car, and they actually paid me to do it!

Disking fields is not very complicated work, it's just back and forth all day long. When you get to one end of the field, you turn around and head back the other way. The hardest part of the job is staying in a straight line. To do that, you need to focus on a tree or fence post off in the distance and head toward it.

Focusing on a long-term goal is also how successful investors stay on track. As we are all aware, financial markets can be very volatile; without a long term perspective, the fear of short-term market fluctuations and the worry of loss can result in poor decision making. A written investment policy statement is the long-range landmark to focus on during hectic times. It outlines your goals and objectives and the strategies for achieving them. In his book, *How to Write an Investment Policy Statement,* Jack Gardner summarizes the practical advantages of an investment policy statement. A well-conceived investment policy statement, writes Gardner, clarifies investment goals and objectives, provides a standard for evaluating investment performance, facilitates clear communication, supports continuity, and protects against capricious and arbitrary decisions.

The clickety-clack of routine can lull you to sleep and cause you to creep into the hot market sectors in the good times, and the sonic blast of a market crash can scare you to death and cause you to swerve out of the market in the bad times. To be a successful investor, you need to ignore market noise — those random short and mid-term fluctuations in prices — and focus on your long-range landmark. An investment policy statement is the landmark that keeps you on track.

Fiduciaries Don't Want to Get Caught With Their Pants Down

"Yeah, but you're not wearing any shorts." That was Coach Miller's reply to Chris when he asked why he got a demerit. Chris always wanted to be the first one in line for our gym class roll call. He would run to class, open his locker, change his clothes, and rush upstairs to the gymnasium, taking the first spot on the painted line. This particular day, Chris was again first in line, so he was the first one that Coach Miller checked to make sure he had followed all the procedures. He was in line within five minutes, his clothes were clean, he was wearing the required reversible t-shirt, and he had this look of pride on his face knowing he had done everything right. That was why Chris was so shocked when Coach Miller said, "one demerit" as he placed a check next to Chris's name on his clipboard list. "Why?" protested Chris, "My Mom washed my clothes!" And that is when Coach Miller uttered the line that went down in infamy for all us sophomore boys in gym class that day. There was Chris — wearing his shirt, shoes, and socks — but no shorts, only a jock strap preserving what dignity he had left.

In Coach Miller's gym class you were not graded on how good an athlete you were, but on how well you knew the rules and followed the procedures. You were given a demerit if you were not dressed and in line within five minutes. You got a demerit if your clothes were not clean, if they were not the standard issue, or if they had any holes in them. You also got demerits for not being in a straight line, for talking, and for slouching. During activities, you were graded on participation and tested on your knowledge of the rules of the different sports, but you were never graded on performance.

Being a fiduciary is a lot like being in Coach Miller's class. You're graded on adherence to a process and not upon results. According to John Langbein, the Reporter for the UPIA, "In drafting the Uniform Prudent Investor Act, we went to extraordinary lengths to remind courts that the standard of prudence is not [portfolio] outcome but [fiduciary] process."

In simple terms, a fiduciary is someone who is responsible for managing someone else's money. The rules on fiduciary conduct, as outlined in Employee Retirement Income Security Act, the Uniform Prudent Investor Act, the Uniform Prudent Management of Institutional Funds Act, and other statutes, are legal defenses for complaints and legal actions taken by the people or institutions whose money is being managed by the fiduciary. Therefore, if a beneficiary is upset with the portfolio's performance but the fiduciary is found to have followed a prudent process, then the fiduciary is not responsible for any losses.

In Coach Miller's class the students could avoid demerits by knowing the rules and following them. It is even more important for fiduciaries to know and follow the rules. According to the Center for Fiduciary Studies (also known as fi360), there are seven common practices for fiduciaries: "(1) Know the standards, laws, and creating document provisions, (2) diversify assets according to the beneficiary's risk and return needs, (3) prepare an investment policy statement, (4) use prudent experts, (5) control and account for expenses, (6) monitor activities, and (7) avoid conflicts of interests and prohibited transactions."

The laws make it clear that a fiduciary is responsible for following a prudent process based on "...the facts and circumstances existing at the time" of a decision and not in hindsight. Therefore, know the rules and diligently follow them because, just like Chris, fiduciaries don't want to get caught with their pants down.

Section 3

Me First: The Consequences of Greed on Wall Street, in Congress, and by Individuals

"To know and not to do is not to know."
- Proverb

Knowing what to do isn't enough. Our country is in a financial mess because as business people, politicians, and individuals, we know what to do but, because of greed, we haven't done it. As a fiduciary, take this to heart: don't let anything get in the way of doing what you know is right.

Welcome to Wall Street's Nightmare

One of my hobbies is working on golf telecasts for the different networks. A few years ago when I was working for CBS at the AT&T Pebble Beach Tournament, there was a backup on the twelfth tee, so I went over and sat on a nearby rock wall to wait for my group's turn to hit. Since I was focused on the golf, I never noticed that another gentleman had joined me on the wall until I felt his hand on my shoulder. I turned and was face to face with one of those famous people you know but don't ever expect to meet. With his left hand still on my shoulder, he stuck out his right hand and said, "Hi, I'm Alice."

Alice Cooper's appearance is a little different, but his manner is very friendly. We sat and talked golf stories and then he shared a very funny story about Groucho Marx. Alice said that after coming home from a concert, he was too wired-up to sleep so he would go next door to his neighbor, Groucho Marx, who had insomnia. They would stay up all night watching old movies. Their friendship grew and the originator of shock rock was, himself, given quite a shock when Groucho showed up at one of his concerts. There, in the middle of the front row, was the octogenarian, Marx, in full tux with his date, Mae West, in her best evening gown.

My surrealistic moment with Alice Cooper got even more dreamlike when his story was interrupted by a very distinctive raspy voice. When I heard "Hello Alice," I didn't have to turn my head to know that Clint Eastwood was standing right next to me.

Cooper, Marx, West, and Eastwood are all very different personalities, but they had one thing in common — carefully crafted public personas created to sell tickets. Cooper, the shock rocker. Marx, the smart aleck. West, the sex symbol. And Eastwood, the tough guy. They all knew that in a world anxious to escape reality, image sells. However, rock stars and movie stars aren't the only ones who know that image sells; Wall Street knows it too, and does it very well. They sold the image and we bought their products. But instead of reaping riches, we found ourselves in a serious financial crisis because, contrary to what they advertised on their websites, Lehman Brothers wasn't "innovative" enough, Merrill Lynch wasn't "smart" enough, Bear Stearns wasn't "strong" enough, Standard and Poors wasn't "independent" enough, and Countrywide said, "yes," too much.

While temporarily escaping reality is the whole point of entertainment, facing reality is how we survive and prosper in life. The reality is that greed and opportunity replaced common sense, judgment, responsibility, and integrity on Wall Street. The *opportunity* was a massive amount of money being generated by the emerging economies in China, India, and elsewhere, looking for a safe place to invest. The *solution* was fixed income securities, ultimately backed by US real estate. The *problem* was the feeding frenzy created to capture all that cash which led to real estate loans being issued without any credit checks. These risky loans were then bundled together and packaged and repacked into various types of interest-bearing securities. In an incredible conflict of interest, the securities were shopped to the various rating agencies, which were more than willing to sell their souls for the right price. Using assumptions that had nothing to do with reality and everything to do with greed, they were able to turn a sow's ear into a silk purse. Backed by these phony ratings and their images as financial experts, Wall Street firms spread this worthless paper all over the world.

In the illusory world of movies, action heroes rule. In the financial world, Wall Street ruled because they were seen as the action heroes. They were James Bond, Indiana Jones, Batman, Iron Man, the Hulk, and Hellboy all rolled into one giant superhero who could provide super returns with no risk. They got this image because the world has come full circle and is coveting the tree of knowledge once more. During the industrial age, power belonged to those who controlled or had access to resources, capital, and infrastructure. As the world shrank, access to information became more important than access to assets. Having assets was not nearly as valuable as identifying who had them and who needed them. In a world with limited resources and unlimited information, power has once more shifted. Since *everyone* has access to information and resources are becoming scarce, the real power is held by those who know how to use information and assets most efficiently and effectively. In this new knowledge age, Wall Street was seen as the holder of financial knowledge.

Unfortunately, Wall Street's image as the financial knowledge expert was no more real than Alice Cooper's shock rock image, but the 'nightmare they welcomed us to'[10] was all too real. Blinded by greed, Wall Street dug a tunnel to riches, and the world rushed in to get the gold. However, in the quest for gold, it is as important to shore up the mine shaft as it is to dig it. Too late, the world found itself in an unstable mine filled with nothing but fool's gold. The ensuing collapse crushed the world's financial markets and the countries, companies, and individuals dependent on them.

The world has learned a harsh lesson. Andre Agassi was wrong when he said in his camera commercials, "Image is everything."[11] With Theodore White's book, *The Making of a President*, we first became aware that TV (and now digital media) have made image more important than substance in the selling of politicians and virtually everything else, including Wall Street, because it is easier to manipulate an image than it is to manipulate reality. Just as a lie repeated enough times becomes accepted as truth, so an image reinforced often enough seems real. And once this image has been accepted as reality, knowledge has a difficult time penetrating the illusion.

Knowledge is impotent against the illusion because we want to believe the image is real. The playwright, George Bernard Shaw, commenting on this phenomenon said, "The moment we want to believe something, we suddenly see all the arguments for it, and become blind to the arguments against it." Even the smartest among us can be blinded to reality as was illustrated by the Congressional testimony of Alan Greenspan, the former Fed Chairman who, when explaining how we got into this mess, used words like "shocked disbelief," "beliefs shaken," "too much faith," "failed to anticipate," "flawed," and, my favorite, "the intellectual edifice collapsed."

The reason the intellectual edifice collapsed is that knowledge alone will never be enough, but knowledge, wisely applied, will. Wikipedia may not be the most authoritative source, but I think they got it just right when they said, "An aspect of knowledge that has been largely forgotten in knowledge economy thinking is wisdom. Wisdom invokes questions of judgment, ethics, experience and intuition, all of which are necessary for the best application of knowledge."[12] Wall Street's image has been tarnished not because it failed, but because it can't be trusted. When I was just starting my career a good friend told me, "Take care of the clients and the money will take care of itself." Wall Street either never knew this or forgot it. Either way, it needs to regain its moral authority or it is in danger of losing its position as the world's financial leader.

If Wall Street is to be trusted again it must not only accept accountability, but also must *seek* it. Boards of directors must stop being sideline cheerleaders and start doing their jobs. They must approve (and actually review) policies and procedures, and they must diligently monitor and evaluate performance. I thought we had learned our lesson with Enron and their 'do-nothing' board, but apparently not. Compensation packages have to be restructured so management is more concerned with long-term sustainability than quarterly profits. The way things stand now, management has every reason to take big risks, because it is rewarded exorbitantly for big short-term profits and fired for trailing the quarterly results of peer companies. And, finally, regulatory audits have to be genuine reviews. Most audits have more to do with determining the organization of a company's paperwork than with the ethics of its behavior or the suitability of its products. These three steps may not cure all of Wall Street's problems, but they are essential emergency measures in controlling the greed that has infected Wall Street.

Entertainers survive and prosper by creating images that are based on their larger-than-life illusions. Wall Street's image cannot be based on illusion because, in the real world, it is impossible to sustain that illusion indefinitely. The only sustainable image is one based on a combination of knowledge, hard work, and integrity; it is called "a good reputation." Wall Street can do it because, as Alexis de Tocqueville observed, "The greatness of America lies not in being more enlightened than any other nation, but rather in her ability to repair her faults."[13]

Washington Has a Higher Credit Limit

"You're kidding me! Jay* only makes half of his lay-ups." Ron's outburst at the basketball awards dinner was so funny because Jay was a cherry picker and everyone knew it. A cherry picker is someone who hangs in the back-court, or fudges that way, in hopes that a missed shot or bad pass will result in a turnover and a long outlet pass, which can be converted into an easy lay-up. Cherry pickers end up padding their own statistics but often hurting their team because of their selfish play. In this case, because of all those lay-ups, Jay got the award for the highest shooting percentage, a little over fifty-percent, even though he was nowhere near the team's best shooter. Ron's comment, while funny, was delivered with a noticeable tinge of sarcasm and anger because Jay was winning awards and getting credit that Ron didn't think he had earned or deserved.

The ability to receive credit for things he hadn't earned is a skill that has served Jay well over the years; you see, Jay is a politician, a very successful and well-known politician. I got to know Jay because he was a hypochondriac. He was positive that he was going to be asphyxiated by the fumes from his roommate's boot polish, so he used to sleep on my dorm room floor.

While lying awake at night, Jay would share his plans to succeed in politics. The plan was to go to a smaller state and start a political action committee and use that as a base to get elected to congress, and from there work his way higher. Over the years I watched in amazement and, I must admit with some jealousy, as his career unfolded as planned.

A few years ago I ended up doing some work with an attorney who had been involved in Jay's political action committee. We were somewhere with a TV when Jay appeared on the screen. I made a comment about him being a college roommate, which wasn't technically true but, like Jay, I wasn't above embellishing a story a little. After hearing my story about Jay's plan, the attorney chuckled and said, "*Now* I understand what was going on." Jay had started the committee and got it going, but once it took off he apparently didn't do much of the work and, as the attorney mentioned, "...he did not seem to care all that much either." The only thing he was really good at was showing up at press conferences and taking credit for, in the words of the attorney, "...things he hadn't done." It seems Jay was still a very good cherry picker.

Not long after that, I was in an airport when I heard, "Guerdon, is that you?" While I hadn't seen Jay in thirty years, I still knew his voice because I had heard it so many times on TV. We talked for about fifteen minutes while his entourage tried to find his limo. As I departed he said, "If you ever need anything, give me a call." I replied, "I don't live in your state, so I can't vote for you." His reply, "In that case, forget it." We both stood there grinning at each other as I thought, "He's the same old cherry picker. If there isn't something in it for him, he's not going to do it."

So what is the point? The point is when our country's economy collapsed, Jay had a major role in Washington's response to the crisis, along with his fellow cherry pickers. Cherry pickers are not only good at taking credit for what they didn't earn, but also for blaming others for problems they may have caused. Washington self-righteously pointed its finger at Wall Street when, in reality, it was just as culpable. The greed and selfish ambition in Washington was every bit as bad as Wall Street's. The only reason Washington wasn't bankrupt along with Wall Street is because Washington has a higher credit limit.

**Names have been changed*

We Want To Need It

"I want it!" my two-year-old niece would say. Her mom would tell her, "You don't need it." To which she would reply, "I *want* to need it." A few years ago, California required you to answer five questions on your driver's license renewal. When I took the application in I was surprised that they didn't grade the test. I asked why and the lady responded, "The law only says you have to take the test, not pass it. So we don't grade it." One summer, my oldest daughter got a job selling home loans and, it appears, the company had a similar method for approving loans. With mortgage and credit card companies not grading the tests, and with all the advertisers telling us we "do" need it, the American consumer went on an "I *want* to need it" spending spree.

How bad the binge has been can be seen by the 2008 statistics on the Grandfather Economic Report website (http://mwhodges.home.att.net). Seventy-nine percent of total debt, both public and private, has been created since 1990 ($45 trillion). The federal government has been totally irresponsible, allowing our national debt to rise to $10.6 trillion. As self-righteous citizens, we were indignant, but we had no right to criticize since our own personal household debt was $13.8 trillion. Maybe we should have listened to our financial advisors and avoided this personal tragedy. The only problem is that our financial institutions were the worst offenders of all with financial sector debt hitting a staggering $17.2 trillion. It's hard for me to imagine, but virtually all the increase in living standard for my baby boomer generation has come from debt. As the website reveals, "...median family incomes stopped growing in 1970 and, thereafter, families tried to keep up by going deeper and deeper into debt ever since (at nearly three times the rate of national economic growth) to an all-time high today."

We can point fingers at the government for taxing and spending, and we can accuse banks of predatory lending, but according to Columbia Business School professor David Beim, "The problem is not the banks [or the government], greedy though they may be, overpaid though they may be. The problem is us... We've been living very high on the hog. Our living standard has been rising dramatically in the last 25 years. And we have been borrowing much of the money to make prosperity happen."[14]

With incomes stagnant, debt soaring, and the savings rate non-existent, we should be arrested for child abuse because we have robbed our kids. I can understand the anger at the AIG bonuses but, unfortunately, we do not have the moral authority to condemn them. They "stole" the taxpayer's money, but we stole from our kids and grandkids. It kind of reminds me of the story in the Bible about King Hezekiah who was told his descendents would be taken into slavery because of his poor decisions. However, he was comfortable with that outcome because, as he put it, "Will there not be peace and security in my lifetime?" Believe it or not, that self-centered jerk was actually considered a "good" king.[15]

Our financial institutions, to misuse a quote by Thomas Friedman, are "...too big to let fail but too stupid to succeed". Our government is riding to the rescue like Don Quixote tilting at windmills, and we, in a paraphrase of Walter Kelly's introduction to the *Best of Pogo*, "...have met the enemy and they are us." We have rewritten the ending to the Declaration of Independence which says "...we mutually pledge to each other our Lives, our Fortunes and our sacred Honor" and replaced it with "...we mutually pledge to our kids the consequences of our Self-Centered lives, our Debts, and our Disgrace." Unfortunately, for the next generation, the "Greatest Generation"[16] has been replaced by the "We Want To Need It Generation."

Section 4

Call to Action: The Duties of a Fiduciary Under the Uniform Prudent Investor Act

"The great end of knowledge is not knowledge, but action."
- Thomas Henry Huxley

The great end of the Uniform Prudent Investor Act ("Act") is prudent actions based on standards promulgated in the Act. In the past, fiduciaries were held responsible for results, but that is no longer the case. In recognition of the uncertainty of life, the Act has made it clear that the standards of prudence are based on actions not outcomes. Therefore, as a fiduciary, your legal liability is determined by how faithfully you fulfill your duties under the Act.

The Risk/Return Tradeoff is the Theme

Whoever said, "Those who can, do, and those who can't, teach," has never been in my wife's third grade class. Doing elementary math, science, history and the rest of the curriculum is a snap, but teaching it to a prepubescent blob of potentiality is way beyond my pay grade. Heck, I don't even know how to access the operating system of a third grader's mind, let alone program it.

Barb, on the other hand, is a magnificent magician who can transform these little minds of mush into masters of multiple academic disciplines. Using a teaching method known as Integrated Thematic Instruction, she weaves together the different subjects based on a year-long theme. So math, science, English, and even music are all integrated around one main theme, which this year is "Building for Success." This theme is not only the central consideration for developing her academic curriculum, but it is also the basis for teaching life skills such as caring, cooperation, friendship, integrity, perseverance, problem solving, and responsibility.

Looking at what she is doing, I realized in many ways, the Uniform Prudent Investor Act is a model of Integrated Thematic Instruction. As has been explained earlier, "The

Uniform Prudent Investor Act undertakes to update trust investment law in recognition of the alterations that have occurred in investment practices." This update was necessary to bring fiduciary practices in line with current economic knowledge "about the behavior of capital markets." It was achieved by altering the criteria for prudent investing from a results standard to a prudent process standard based on "the main theme of modern investment practice, sensitivity to the risk/return [tradeoff]."

This theme is integrated into a prudent process in subsections (a) and (b) of Section 2, with the requirement that the risk/return tradeoff is considered when:

1. Defining objectives reasonably suited to the trust,
2. Establishing an overall investment strategy,
3. Determining the purposes, terms, distributions requirements, and other circumstances of the trust,
4. Exercising reasonable care, skill, and caution, and
5. Evaluating individual assets in the context of the [investment] portfolio as a whole.

At the heart of Barb's program are behavioral guidelines for classroom conduct. Students are expected to use these guidelines in their daily interactions and they are held accountable to them throughout their entire school experience. Likewise at the heart of the Uniform Prudent Investor Act are duties that make up a prudent investment process. Fiduciaries are expected to follow this process and if they don't they can be held liable for any investment losses.

"Building for Success" is the theme for Barb's students and "The tradeoff between risk and return is identified as the fiduciary's [main theme and] central consideration." The school's curriculum and the behavioral guidelines for students are woven into their theme, just as the standards of the law and the duties of fiduciaries are woven into the theme of the Uniform Prudent Investor Act. With this in mind, notice as you read through the fables in this section how the risk/ return tradeoff influences the duties and responsibilities of fiduciaries.

If a Fiduciary Isn't Careful, He Will End Up on a Wild Goose Chase

"You're facing them the wrong way and the sentries should be on the outside." Nobody likes being bossed around by his brother, especially on a cold, drizzly winter morning, but I wasn't stupid enough to ignore orders from the best hunter I knew. If I wanted to get any good hunting in, I'd better listen to what he was saying.

My brother, Frank, had me set out the goose decoys in a U-shaped pattern, in groups of five or so to resemble families, and with the sentries on the edges. Our decoys had heads that were attached through a hole in the neck of the body to a frame by large rubber bands that we had made out of old inner tubes. We had two types of heads: feeders and sentries. The feeder heads curved down toward the ground to make the decoys look like they were eating, and the sentry heads stood straight up to look like they were on watch. We had mostly feeders and only a few sentries, because too many sentries would signal danger and spook the geese we were trying to attract.

While I was putting out the decoys, Frank fixed up our hunting blind. A blind is just what the name implies: you want to make it so you are unseen by the geese. That means not only blending into the surroundings, but as Frank said,

"You want to put it in a place where the geese won't be looking;" how he knew where *that* might be, I had no clue.

Dad used to say that Frank was a good goose hunter because he thought like a goose, but I disagreed — I always thought Frank was a real turkey. Frank seemed to enjoy figuring out how to set out decoys so they looked natural to the birds flying over. He was very careful, methodical, and observant. Preparing for the hunt seemed almost more enjoyable to him than the actual hunt. I, on the other hand, just liked to blast away. Sort of like that guy in the Alice's Restaurant song[17] jumping up and down and yelling "I want to kill," I wanted action, not "careful."

Being careful, methodical, and observant are not only important attributes for a prudent fiduciary, but also requirements of law. The Uniform Prudent Investor Act includes *the duty of care* as one of the requirements of a prudent fiduciary. According to the comments in Section 227 of the Prudent Investor Rule, "The duty of care requires the trustee to exercise reasonable effort and diligence in making and monitoring investments for the trust, with attention to the trust's objectives."

Therefore, for a fiduciary, the starting point when managing assets for an individual or an organization is to determine the objectives of that person or entity. For an individual, an important objective may be "to retire by age 65;" for a charity, an objective may be "to maintain the level of programs and services." For us, as hunters, the objective was to shoot geese. To achieve their objectives, both a hunter and a prudent fiduciary need to carefully analyze the situation and then diligently develop, implement, and monitor an appropriate plan.

My brother made the effort to observe how geese behave and then took the time to develop a plan that mimicked such behavior. It was my job to carefully place the decoys according to the plan. If the decoys didn't work, we would modify the decoy pattern or move the hunting blind until we got a setup that achieved our objective of attracting birds. A fiduciary must also go through these same steps when developing and monitoring a beneficiary's investment plan, because if a fiduciary isn't careful, he will end up on a wild goose chase.

Fiduciaries, Like Fly Fishers, Develop Their Skills

If golf is, as the book title says, *A Good Walk Spoiled*, then stream fly fishing is a good walk improved. I was never as crazy about fishing as my Dad and brother, and I hated lake fishing, but I did genuinely enjoy stream fly fishing. We fished quite a few different streams over the years. The Deschutes River in Central Oregon was probably the best. It had a native trout called the Redside; if you've ever seen one, you'd know how it got its name. The Deschutes was a fun stream with big fish, but it wasn't my favorite spot — that distinction was reserved for Stony Creek.

Most everyone who fished the Middle Fork of Stony Creek would drive to Red Bridge and fish up to the gorge. We, on the other hand, drove up the opposite ridgeline and dropped down Bear Wallow Creek into Stony Creek above the gorge. It was a hard, steep, vegetation-choked, five-mile hike, but it had two benefits. We loved the hike and, since no one else did, we usually had the stream to ourselves.

Stream fly fishing requires a fair amount of skill. You want to present the fly to the fish without spooking them and in such a way that it looks natural. That means avoiding splashing the line over the top of the fish, and making sure the line is not so tense as to drag the fly unnaturally across the surface instead of letting it drift normally with the current. Since trout usually congregate at the head of a pool, you need to throw the line in the fast water upstream and let it drift down into the pool. To ensure the fly drifts naturally, you must keep a gentle curve in the line with enough slack so that there are a few tiny waves in it. The trick is to have just enough tension on the line so you can feel any hits, but not so much that it drifts unnaturally. Learning the technique for throwing the line in an open area is hard enough, but doing it in the restricted space of a densely forested small stream is almost impossible. It's like trying to throw a curve ball from inside a phone booth.

Over the years I developed some skill at fly fishing because I was taught by my Dad and brother, and because I practiced. Skill is defined in the dictionary as "...a proficiency, facility, or dexterity that is acquired or developed through training and experience."[18] Since, according to the comments sections of the Prudent Investor Rule, a fiduciary is "...liable for losses resulting from the failure to use the skill of an individual of ordinary intelligence," it is mandatory that the fiduciary develops his or her skill at investing and managing the investments of his or her clients, beneficiaries, or participants. Just as an individual of ordinary ability can learn to be very proficient at fly fishing, so can an individual of ordinary intelligence learn to be proficient at managing and investing the assets of a person, trust, or pension for which her or she is responsible. Therefore, a fiduciary cannot use inexperience as an excuse since he is held to the level of skill he could acquire as an ordinary person, if he worked at developing those skills.

However, no matter how hard one works, the Uniform Prudent Investor Act recognizes that it may be prudent to delegate investment and management decisions to an agent possessing specific "professional skills or facilities." Years ago, when I was working on a thoroughbred ranch, the manager was taking a horseshoeing class. When I asked him why he was doing it, since it would be nuts for him to attempt to shoe one of these multi-million dollar horses, he replied, "Of course I'm not going to shoe any of these horses, but I want to be able to tell if the ones doing it are doing it right." Even if a fiduciary delegates investment decision making to an experienced professional, that does not relieve the fiduciary from the duty to monitor. And that requires skill along with knowledge and diligence. Fly fishing is hard and being a fiduciary is hard. To do either "right," one must take the time and effort to develop one's skills.

Fiduciaries, Like Hunters, Exercise Extreme Caution

"Go stand in the corner." "What for? It was only the barrel," I protested, knowing it was an argument I wasn't going to win. I had just broken my dad's number one gun rule: 'Know where your gun barrel is pointed at all times.' And, by inference, it should never be pointed at another person, even if it's not loaded, even if the safety is on and — in this case — even if it was broken down for cleaning and it was only a barrel without the chamber or magazine attached.

Since hunting involves a loaded weapon, it is inherently risky. Therefore, a cautious hunter always follows a set of gun safety rules. My brother and I learned these rules from our Dad. The first thing we did when picking up a gun was to check to see if it was loaded. Even after confirming that it wasn't, we were taught to still treat it as if it were. We never stored or transported a loaded gun and it remained empty until we were in the field ready to hunt. Once it was loaded, the safety was always on until the gun was shouldered and ready to fire.

Investing is also inherently risky. In his book on the Uniform Prudent Investor Act, W. Scott Simon says, "...there is no panacea for investing. Because risk is risk there's no guaranteed safe way to reap the rewards of investing in financial markets." In recognition of this risk, the Uniform Prudent Investor Act requires fiduciaries, like hunters, to follow a set of rules. At the heart of these rules is the Prudent Investor Rule which requires a fiduciary to "...invest and manage trust assets as a prudent investor would, by considering the purposes, terms, distribution requirements, and other circumstances of the trust [and] in satisfying this standard, [to] exercise reasonable care, skill, and caution."

While the general safety rules of hunting never changed, the gun selection, its set up and the type of shells used varied depending on the type of hunting and the size, strength, and skill level of the hunter. For example, my favorite gun was a 20-gauge Remington Model 17. Since it was lightweight, it was a great gun for pheasant and dove hunting, but its smaller bore made it less compatible with the large shot and higher shot speed required for goose hunting. The 12-gauge Browning A5 was a better gun for goose hunting. However, when I first started hunting I was too small to handle the Browning so, based on the circumstances, a cautious trade-off between risk and reward required me to use the 20-gauge.

Circumstances also determine how a fiduciary balances the risk and return needs of a beneficiary's portfolio. Caution would dictate that, for an elderly person with significant distributions needs, the investment portfolio should focus on safety of principal. For a younger person with little need for distributions, a cautious fiduciary would be more concerned about the long-term detrimental effect of inflation and would, therefore, allocate a significantly larger portion of the portfolio to stocks and other equities.

Hunters have a set of gun safety rules to minimize the dangers to themselves and those around them in order to reduce the risk of a horrible accident. Fiduciaries go through a prudent process for the same reason: to minimize the dangers to their trust, charitable, or pension beneficiaries and the liabilities to themselves. Situations come up in a hunt where a cautious hunter needs to determine if a risk is worth taking. In the same way, a cautious fiduciary weighs the risks and returns based on the beneficiary's circumstances to determine if a risk is worth taking. Hunting and investing are both dangerous activities, so fiduciaries (like hunters) must exercise extreme caution.

Fiduciaries, Like Beekeepers, Make Moves with the Big Picture in Mind

We called him High-Pockets. Like most good nicknames, we didn't consciously set out to create one, it just happened. High-Pockets was really tall. One day, a co-worker off-handedly observed, "Gee, you have high pockets," and it stuck. High-Pockets and a dozen or so other individuals made up the cast of characters employed by Wenner Honey Farms, a six thousand hive operation that made most of its money from selling bees, not honey. We sold about 20,000 two-pound packages of bees and 60,000 queens each year. At this point, you are probably trying to figure out, "How do you weigh bees?" and "How do you get them into a package?" The package was placed on a scale and we shook bees into it from a wire cage. We got the bees into the cage by driving them out of their hives with a foul smelling substance called *Bee-Go*. The work wasn't too bad but it had a detrimental effect on your social life because you couldn't wash the *Bee-Go* smell off your body. Even after showering with the hottest water and harshest soap, you still smelled like you'd just fallen into an outhouse pit. I remember sitting in church and noticing that everyone around was looking the bottoms of their shoes. So I checked mine, shrugged my shoulders and pretended I didn't know where the smell was coming from either.

In addition to selling bees, we also rented out hives for pollination and sold honey. To accommodate these activities, each one of the six thousand hives was moved four or five times a year. Before I came along, there was no overall plan in place for moving hives. Each move was "planned" based on what seemed like a good idea at the time, without considering the long-term consequences of that action. It was a very inefficient and costly system.

When I took over, I set up a cohesive strategy where moves were not made in isolation but in the context of an overall plan. I saw the operation as a one-year repetitive cycle, where all the hives started in "winter" yards, moved to the almond orchards for pollination in February, and then split in all different directions after that. The ones with specialty queens went to "nuc" yards, basically bee brothels, so that the drones (male bees) from those hives could mate with the new queens hatching in the small shoebox-size hives called "nucs." Other hives were moved into the hills for Manzanita honey and some went into the prunes for pollination. Later in the summer, there were alfalfa, cotton, and vine seed pollinations, in addition to our star-thistle honey yards. By keeping track of the specialty hives and the progression of all hives into various locations, I was able to greatly reduce the average distance of each move and even the number of moves, significantly decreasing the annual man hours and truck miles required for moving bees.

Just like hive moving, investment decisions should not be made in isolation. The standard of prudence requires that a fiduciary's "...investment and management decisions respecting individual assets must be evaluated not in isolation but in the context of the trust portfolio..." That means the investment portfolio must be properly diversified, taking into account all trust assets including "...financial assets, interests in closely held enterprises, tangible and intangible personal property, and real property." For example, if the beneficiary already owns a significant amount of real estate, it probably isn't wise to put more real estate into the investment portfolio. If most of the trust assets are illiquid, the investment portfolio should be more liquid. If there are both income and remainder beneficiaries, it needs to be determined if generating income is more important than growing capital. A fiduciary needs to know who he or she is working for, what are the beneficiary's needs and wants, and then figure out how to do it. The key is always having an eye on the big picture so you know *why* you are doing *what* you are doing.

Looking at the overall plan saved my bee boss a lot of headaches and even more money. When the focus is moved from the action in isolation to the action in relationship to the whole, what originally seemed imprudent may actually be prudent and, conversely, the prudent may become imprudent. So fiduciaries, like beekeepers, need to make moves with the big picture in mind.

Risk Tolerance Should Be Based On Circumstances, Not Testosterone Levels

"That's the girls' platform. Go to the top." That taunt challenged the budding masculinity of this ten-year-old boy, forcing me to climb the wooden rungs up past the second platform, to the third and highest one. Looking down from the ten-foot-high structure and then fifteen more feet of creek bank, it felt like I was standing on top of the world — and it was *not* a good feeling. I had a choice: did I swing across the creek on the rope or did I go back down and face eternal shame? If they ever make a dumb pill, I am convinced the active ingredient will be testosterone because I jumped — even though I was positive that it meant certain death. Well, I didn't die, but I did have a death grip on the rope so that when I reached the other side, I didn't let go. Unfortunately, the return trip was on a different path which was taking me straight toward the trunk of the old oak tree from which the rope was suspended. My brain knew to let go, but fear kept that message from being received by my hands. The force with which I hit the tree was, however, sufficient to loosen my grip. Like a pinball I bounced off the tree, ricocheted off the bank, and face-planted into the muddy waters of the creek. Resembling *The Creature from the Black Lagoon,*[19] I rose from the mud and climbed the bank to face the howls of laughter from my friends and from the creator of this death trap, Ernie.

Ernie was the only adult we called by his first name. He may have been the only adult, other than our parents, whose given name we even knew. Ernie was an optical illusion. You knew he was old, but your eyes wouldn't let your mind believe it. He was in his seventies but he looked like Charles Atlas with his cut-off pants and his sleeveless shirts. He was so strong that he only held the rope in one hand and could do stunts that no one else would dare attempt.

Climbing the tree to hang the rope was something very few people would have the courage to do, but Ernie had a very high tolerance for risk. His risk tolerance did not seem to be at all tempered by either age or circumstances, a luxury most fiduciaries don't have. As the Uniform Prudent Investor Act notes, "Returns correlate strongly with risk, but tolerance for risk varies greatly with the financial and other circumstances of the investor, or in the case of a trust, with the purposes of the trust and the relevant circumstances of the beneficiaries." The Act implies that time-horizon, income needs, and financial well-being are three important circumstances to be considered, because "...a trust whose main purpose is to support an elderly widow of modest means will have a lower risk tolerance than a trust to accumulate for a young scion of great wealth."

Most people think of risk tolerance in subjective terms, the amount of loss an investor can emotionally handle; however, the guidance in the Act stresses that risk tolerance should be objectively determined based on circumstances. But I have observed that both amateur and professional investors tend to assume more risk in good markets and less risk in bad markets. For example, in the late 1990s there was a lot of pressure to take on inappropriate risk in order to match the returns of the dot-com sector. This led to inappropriate portfolio asset allocations and a tendency to make hasty changes when unexpected returns were realized.

As a young boy, I sometimes took inappropriate risks because "everyone else was doing it" or because I felt like I had to prove my masculinity. However, since fiduciaries are managing someone else's money, they cannot make decisions based on feelings, emotions, or opinions. Fiduciaries must, instead, make prudent decisions about risk tolerance based on objective factors, the needs and circumstances of their beneficiaries, and not on peer pressure or testosterone levels or any other subjective factors.

Time-Horizons Can Always Change Because Circumstances Change

"My most important short-term goal is this month's rent payment and my most important long-term goal is next month's," I replied to a question from my wife. She had been at a conference where the homework was to ask your spouse their most important short and long-term objectives. At the time, we were a struggling young family and my statement was not too far from the truth. Things were so tight that a big night out was splitting a turkey sandwich and a cup of soup at Denny's, and then going window-shopping at the grocery store.

According to the Center for Fiduciary Studies, a person's time-horizon is characterized by "...that point-in-time when more money is flowing out of the portfolio than is coming in from contributions and /or from portfolio growth," If that is true, then our time-horizon was short and getting shorter. The plan was for my wife to support us while I went back to school to get a master's degree in business. So much for plans; by the time school started, Barb had been laid off and was pregnant, so I had to get a job. I sacked grain at a local mill in the mornings and worked in the school's computer lab in the evening. With those two jobs, a full load of graduate studies, a new wife, and a baby on the way, I was tapped out.

I knew what my time-horizon was: it was two years until graduation. Fiduciaries also need to know their time-horizons. While the Uniform Prudent Investor Act does not mention time-horizon specifically, it is implicit in the requirement that fiduciaries develop "...an overall investment strategy having risk and return objectives reasonably suited to the trust, [pension, or charity]." As an experienced financial advisor, I have found that figuring out a suitable time-horizon is the most difficult task and the most important factor in determining an appropriate balance between fixed income and stock investments.

For short-term portfolios, safety of principal is most important. Therefore, the balance between fixed income and stocks should be weighted more toward fixed income, and the fixed income should be short in maturity and high in quality to further reduce volatility. As Will Rogers once said, "I'm more concerned with the return 'of' my money than the return 'on' my money." With longer-term portfolios, the Act warns about "the possible effect of inflation" as a risk factor, which generally would require moving the weightings toward stocks. So, determining the correct time-horizon and matching it with an appropriate investment allocation is important because, as the Center for Fiduciary Studies points out, "An investment strategy can fail by being too conservative as well as too aggressive."

Life is full of all kinds of time-horizons. At school, I had the two-year time-horizon. In the computer science lab, I had a one semester time-horizon for the students' business simulation games. At the mill, we had seasonal time-horizons where the supply and demand for feeds had to be matched. Being pregnant, Barb had a nine month time-horizon. In each case, circumstances determined the time-horizon. The Act recognizes this fact and requires that

"...among circumstances that a [fiduciary] shall consider in investing and managing [portfolio] assets are...the need for liquidity, regularity of income, and preservation or appreciation of capital..."

As I get older my time-horizons don't necessarily get shorter. We now have enough income and savings so that our investment time-horizon extends beyond next month's housing payment to include the lives of our grandchildren. However, in an uncertain world, time-horizons can always change because circumstances change.

Fiduciaries Need to Monitor What They Manage and the Agents to Whom They Delegate

"You're not supposed to sit on the tables." The words are a statement but the tone was an order. I looked down at the little four-year-old bug and thought about telling him to buzz off but, since this was my first time in my new girlfriend's preschool, I figured I'd better not cause problems. Obediently I stood up, to the smug delight of the little munchkin who reminded me of one of those lollipop boys from *The Wizard of Oz*[20], with the way he talked out of the side of his mouth.

Going into my future wife's preschool was like entering Munchkin Land. The room was all bright primary colors and everything was in miniature: the tables, chairs, bookshelves, coat rack, and even the people. And in the middle of this miniature world stood Barb; with her auburn hair and ivory skin she was a real life Glinda. It was so Oz-like I expected her to break out in song: "Come out, come out wherever you are and meet the young [man] who fell from a star. [He] fell from the sky, [he] fell very far and [Ord Bend he] says is the name of the star."

Ord Bend wasn't really a star, it was not much more than a little general store located near a bend in the Sacramento

River, in the middle of orchard and row crop farms. My place was a shack that looked a lot like Dorothy's house after the tornado hit it. Because I was tending bees in the area around where Barb's preschool was located, I had a chance to stop by quite a bit. I don't remember many of the names, but the cast of characters was impossible to forget. The little lollipop kid never did like me. I think he'd marked his territory and he didn't want any other alpha males intruding. There was also the little drummer boy who kept a constant background beat going on whatever flat surface he could find. But my favorite was Merlin, who spoke in his own language that was completely indecipherable. It was like he was chanting incantations from the real Merlin the Magician.

To paraphrase the intro to *The Naked City*[21], "There were twenty-five kids in The Munchkin City and each one of them had a story." Barb knew that not only did her kids have different personalities but also different learning styles and different stages of development and, in some cases, behavioral and developmental disabilities. Good curriculum was important in helping her kids learn, develop, and manage any difficulties, but the curriculum had to be adapted to the needs of each kid and not the other way around. So she started by screening and testing to determine appropriate activities and programs for each child, and followed up by monitoring to determine the ongoing suitability of those programs. When she ran into difficult situations, she got assistance from the experts at the county's mental health department.

Similarly, fiduciaries not only need to design portfolios that are appropriate for each individual beneficiary but they also need to monitor them on an ongoing basis. According to the Uniform Prudent Investor Act, the duty to monitor embraces the "...trustee's continuing responsibility for oversight of the suitability of investments already made as well as the trustee's decisions respecting new investments." And when fiduciaries find that it is prudent to delegate some of their responsibilities to trained professional agents, the delegation doesn't relieve fiduciaries of their responsibility to review "...the agent's actions in order to monitor the agent's performance and compliance with the terms of the delegation."

As a responsible preschool teacher, Barb monitored the performance of her kids and the activities of the experts who assisted her. Likewise, to determine the ongoing suitability of investments, fiduciaries need to monitor what they manage and the agents to whom they delegate.

Fiduciaries, Like Spotters, Have a Duty to Investigate

"You had better be right or don't bother coming in." Those were about half the words Chuck Will, the long time producer of CBS golf telecasts, screamed in my headset as I stood on the side of the 18th green at Sahalee Country Club. It was near the end of the second round of the 1998 PGA Championship and I had just radioed the production trailer that Kevin Sutherland's putt was for a bogey, not par, as the announcer had just said. Chuck had come back with his expletive-loaded statement to inform me that whatever score Sutherland got was going to be the cut line for the tournament. "Was I sure?", because they were going with my call. It was actually a really big deal since getting it wrong would expose the network to the ridicule of their rivals in the print media. With conviction in my voice and doubt in my mind I said, "I'm sure."

I had been hired, along with some of my buddies, as spotters for the Thursday and Friday rounds. Spotters are the eyes and ears of the production crew. We were out on the course helping the people in the trailers make sense of the limited information available on their monitors, by providing information on yardages, club selection, hitting order, and shots played. We were the B Team working the weekdays that would be replaced by the A Team on the weekend. The A Team usually consisted of caddies whose players didn't make the cut, so they were free on Saturdays and Sundays. Caddies make great spotters because they are very good at accurately gathering the information needed by the producer and directors to put together a good telecast.

However, they decided to keep me and my buddies for the weekend because of the good work we had done and because I got the big call right. I got it right because I took the time to investigate Kevin Sutherland's situation. When you are spotting, the producer will call and ask for information on players who are in the hunt. Since John Cook was the only one in my group having a good day, all my calls had been requests for information on "Cookie." On eighteen, Sutherland drove his ball into the woods on the right, while Cook was in the fairway. I wanted to get Cook's yardage because I was sure I would get a call on him, but I also had a duty to investigate what was going on with Sutherland. So I headed into the woods and watched as he "wasted" a shot in the soft pine needles. Not having seen the missed shot, the on-course announcer relayed erroneous information that could have caused real embarrassment if I hadn't corrected it.

Just like a spotter, a fiduciary has a "duty to investigate." According to the Uniform Prudent Investor Act, "...a [fiduciary] shall make a reasonable effort to verify facts relevant to the investment and management of [portfolio] assets." The Act explains that a fiduciary investor has a responsibility "to examine information likely to bear importantly on the value or the security of an investment." That means a fiduciary needs to investigate records of title, have land appraised, reject unaudited financial statements, and perform a thorough analysis of any data that would relate to the stability or authenticity of an investment. In performing this due diligence, a fiduciary not only needs to examine potential investments but also determine if they match the time-horizon, risk tolerance, and needs of the client, beneficiary, charity or other entity.

A fiduciary who performed an appropriate investigation would have protected his or her beneficiary from the fraud of Bernie Madoff, the deceit of the Stanford Group, the concentration of Bill Miller's mutual fund, the lack of transparency of hedge funds, or the high costs of many annuities. It took effort to check out Kevin Sutherland's situation and it takes effort to check out investment choices. As it turned out, though I didn't know it at the time, Sutherland's wasted shot in the woods was the most important stroke of the day. Just because you never know, both a spotter and a fiduciary have a duty to investigate.

Portfolios, Like Families, Are Made Up Of Pieces That Fit Together Well

I've heard it said that "family is when you have no place else to go, they have to take you in." I'd change that to "they have to *consider* taking you." I know that in my family there have been some questions about the legitimacy of my own membership, especially among my kids. Once, when my middle daughter, Anna, was about seven or eight, we were looking for a family dog. Anna wanted a Saint Bernard because of the Beethoven movies. My wife was reluctant because her college roommate had had one. She told Anna, "They are very nice dogs but they drool a lot and fart all the time." Sweet little Anna replied in all honesty, "Well so does Dad, but we keep him." I think if we had held a family vote at the time, the kids would have voted me out and the Saint Bernard in.

Having three daughters and no sons, I often feel like Rodney Dangerfield; they may accept me as their dad, but I don't get any respect. When they were kids they would sit around the dinner table telling "blond" jokes which they turned into "dad' jokes. What was really sad was that they couldn't even compliment me when they tried. My oldest, Sarah, had just broken up with a long-time boyfriend and was a little bit distraught when she told me, "I've had it with good-looking, athletic men. I want to marry someone just like you Dad." Sadly, I had to rely on my youngest, Hillary, to get any sort of revenge. I always referred to her as the "Peanut Princess" so she called me "King Daddy" and her mother "Queen Mommy." One day Sarah asked Hillary, "If you are a princess, and mom and dad are king and queen, then who are Anna and me?" Without missing a beat Hillary replied, "You're the two ugly step-sisters."

With all of our craziness, we are a healthy family because each one of us plays a role that contributes to the well-being of our family. We are each very different, but we fit together in a way that makes us better than the sum of our individual parts. Investment portfolios are very much like families; some are healthy, and some are dysfunctional. A portfolio is healthy when, according to the Uniform Prudent Investor Act, each investment "plays an appropriate role in achieving the risk/return objective of the [portfolio]." Some investments may seem inherently inappropriate when viewed by themselves but, just like me and my odd quirks add value to our family, these seemingly inappropriate investments add value to a portfolio.

The Act puts it this way, "Specific investments or techniques are not *per se* prudent or imprudent. The riskiness of a specific property, and thus the propriety of its inclusion in the trust estate, is not judged in the abstract but in terms of its anticipated effect on the particular trust's portfolio... The premise... is that trust beneficiaries are better protected by the Act's emphasis on close attention to risk/return objectives... than in attempts to identify categories of investment that are *per se* prudent or imprudent." The law refers to this as "abrogating categoric restrictions." When my daughters started dating I called it "not rejecting the boy until you got to know him." Traditional trust law was encumbered with a variety of categoric exclusions, such as prohibitions on junior mortgages or new ventures. In some states, legislation created so-called "legal lists" of approved trust investments. Can you image if I had tried to put together a "legal list" of approved boyfriends?

We do not have the perfect family, and I have never seen a perfect portfolio. But we *are* a healthy family that can handle its problems because we fit together well. Similarly, a portfolio is healthy if it fits together well. Therefore, building a portfolio, like building a family, is not about trying to find the perfect pieces but about fitting together different pieces to complete the picture.

Professional Fiduciaries, Like Professional Golfers, Are Expected To Have Greater Skills

If you read Michener's *Texas* you might remember that one defense for murder was to claim the victim was a "low-life duck sluicer," (someone who shoots ducks while they are sitting on a pond or the ground.) In golf, a sandbagger is akin to a duck sluicer. A sandbagger is someone who creates an artificially high handicap to have a better chance of winning tournaments. Accusing a duck hunter of sluicing or a golfer of sandbagging is, in the words of Shakespeare, "the most unkindest cut of all."

The average golfer has a handicap of 16, which means the average score is about 16 strokes over par. Less than one-percent of golfers have handicaps under ten but professional golfers are such experts that they actually have negative handicaps, their average scores are under par. As in all sports, the difference between amateur and professional golfers is huge. Golf is unique however, by virtue of the fact that the skill difference can be quantified because you are playing the course instead of playing another person. This uniqueness allows golfers of different skill levels to fairly compete against each other, as long as they are not sandbaggers. Therefore, I can play against my brother-in-law, who is a professional golfer, even though he is a much better golfer than I, because our scores are adjusted for our handicaps.

In its own way, the Uniform Prudent Investor Act handicaps fiduciaries. "The prudent investor standard applies to a range of fiduciaries, from the most sophisticated professional investment management firms and corporate fiduciaries [low-handicappers], to family members of minimal experience [high-handicappers]." Just as the standards are higher for professional golfers, so are they for professional fiduciaries. As the Act continues, "Because the standard of prudence is relational, it follows that the standard for professional trustees is the standard of prudent professionals; for amateurs, it is the standard of prudent amateurs." There was some discussion whether to exempt small trusts from the prudent investor rule, but it was decided that the distinction between standards for amateur versus professional fiduciaries was enough to ease the burden of compliance for small trusts.

Because higher standards are required of professional fiduciaries, the Act does not allow reverse sandbagging. "The trustee is under a duty to the beneficiary in administering the trust to exercise such care and skill as a man of ordinary prudence would exercise in dealing with his own property; and if the trustee has or procures his appointment as trustee by representing that he has greater skill than that of a man of ordinary prudence, he is under a duty to exercise such skill." In other words, if a fiduciary uses a claim of greater skill to obtain a position as trustee, then that fiduciary had better have those skills and had better use them.

A professional golfer like my brother-in-law is expected to shoot around 70 because he has a minus two handicap. I, on the other hand, am only expected to shoot around 82 because my handicap is ten. Just as the standards for professional and amateur golfers are different, so are the standards for professional and amateur fiduciaries different because of the different levels of skill. Note that the standards are different for *skill* but not for *care*, because both the professional and amateur fiduciaries are required to administer trust assets with the same care and skill they would "exercise in dealing with [their] own property." Put simply, both professional and amateur fiduciaries are to treat the trust property as if it were their own, but professional fiduciaries (and pro golfers) are expected to have greater skill than a person of ordinary prudence (and a golfer of ordinary ability).

The Dangers of Concentration and the Duty to Diversify

"I want my daddy." When my big sister was a little girl, all she had to do was pick up the phone and ask and she would be magically connected with our Dad. It wasn't some kind of modern voice recognition phone equipment, it was small town America in the 1940s. The little town of Forest Hill had its own phone company that was owned and operated by Mr. and Mrs. Hoeper. With only about 500 customers, Mrs. Hoeper, who ran the switchboard from her living room, knew every voice in town. She was a real-life Ernestine, comedian Lily Tomlin's alter ego telephone operator.

By the time I was born, our family had moved to the farm town of Willows. It wasn't much more than a gas and bus stop along Highway 99W. It didn't have its own phone company but it did have its own cheese factory (Rumiano Cheese Company), its own butcher shop (Weinrich Meat Shop), its own bakery, and its own grocery store (SaniFood Market) — all of which sold locally grown and raised products. In addition, it had a locally owned bank (First National Bank of Willows) and even its own radio station. The station was so small-town that our local weatherman made *WKRP in Cincinnati's* Les Nessman look professional.[22] His weather report consisted of giving the temperature and then opening the window to determine if it was windy, cloudy, or raining.

In the last few years of his life, my father started to decry the loss of small town diversity. Looking at our economy through the eyes of a biologist, he would say it was becoming a monoculture. A salmonella outbreak in the past used to affect a city or county, now it affects the whole country because there are no longer thousands of local slaughterhouses, only a few very large regional ones. Similarly, a glitch in a satellite, a truckers' strike, or bad bank loans cause problems nationally instead of just locally.

Monocultures are not only breeding grounds for massive food-borne disasters, but also a recipe for the collapse of investment portfolios. To reduce the likelihood of a financial disaster, the Uniform Prudent Investor Act reminds us "...prudent investing ordinarily requires diversification." It explains the rationale for diversification by pointing out that "Diversification reduces risk... [because] stock price movements are not uniform. They are imperfectly correlated. This means that if one holds a well-diversified portfolio, the gains in one investment will cancel out the losses in another... For example, during the Arab oil embargo of 1973, international oil stocks suffered declines, but the shares of domestic oil producers and coal companies benefited. Holding a broad enough portfolio allowed the investor to offset, to some extent, the losses associated with the embargo... [Therefore], as long as stock prices do not move exactly together, the risk of a diversified portfolio will be less than the average risk of the separate holdings." As a practical means to achieve diversification, especially for small trusts, the Act encourages pooling investment vehicles or "...investing in mutual funds," to lower costs and increase efficiency.

In Forest Hill, a phone outage was local and usually caused by a falling tree or Mrs. Hoeper leaving her switchboard to visit the bathroom. Modern telecommunications are more efficient but concentration has made it more vulnerable to catastrophes. Recent events have also exposed the problems of concentration in financial institutions and food processing plants. Fiduciaries need to take note of the dangers of concentration and heed the Uniform Prudent Investor Act's requirement to diversify their portfolios.

Sometimes Special Circumstances are More Important than Diversification

I had a highly skilled job that involved a wheelbarrow and a shovel. I was the relief poop scooper on weekends for a thoroughbred horse ranch in the hills east of Santa Barbara. I was told that the ranch was owned by an heiress to the Champion Sparkplug fortune, but I don't know for sure since I never saw her. All I knew was it was managed by a man and woman from my home town.

It was a great job for a college student; besides my pay it included free meals and a free room in the pool house that was a mansion compared to my dorm room. It was also a humbling experience; not the job itself but the realization that the horses were considered more valuable and less expendable than myself. On my first day, I opened the gate and headed into the stall of one of the stallions. The foreman came running over and jerked me out, screaming, "Are you nuts? You could have been killed. Let us get the stallions out before you go in." I thanked him for his concern and he replied, "I don't give a damn about you, I just don't want one of these million-dollar horses getting hurt while they are stomping you to death." The scary part was he wasn't joking. The *really* scary part was you could sense the horses felt the same way. On the ranch I was low man (or should I say mammal) on the totem pole, with the other people, horses, and even the dogs and cats considered more valuable than me.

The horses had a "special value" to the owner, the riders, and the people working on the ranch beyond their monetary value. A horse can be monetarily valued by a qualified appraiser who, according to Wikipedia, will consider objective standards, "...such as conformation, disposition, training level, pedigree, intellect and temperament." In addition, the horse's health, soundness, breed, color, age, and sex are all important considerations in the valuation of a horse. But as they also point out, "A horse is a unique individual and sometimes impossible to value."

When managing assets, fiduciaries are required to be objective — but they are also required to consider unique and sometimes hard to value intangibles. The Uniform Prudent Investor Act instructs fiduciaries to consider "...an asset's special relationship or special value, if any, to the purposes of the trust or to one or more of the beneficiaries." While diversification is one of the most important concepts of prudent investing, the Act makes it clear that "...circumstances can, however, overcome the duty to diversify." According to the Act one such situation is "...the wish to retain a family business."

If the trust is silent, the decision to retain the special value asset is up to the fiduciary. As the Act points out, "A trustee shall diversify the investments of the trust unless the trustee reasonably determines that, because of special circumstances, the purposes of the trust are better served without diversifying." Therefore, to make this decision the fiduciary not only needs to consider the importance of a special asset to an individual but also the purposes of the trust. I believe the best guidance for this situation is found in the *Restatement (Third) of Trusts (Prudent Investor Rule)*

Commentary, "The trustee's decision to retain or dispose of certain assets may properly be influenced, even without trust terms expressly bearing on the decision, by the property's special relationship to some objective of the settlor that may be inferred from the circumstances or by some special interest or value the property may have as a part of the trust or that it may have, consistent with the trust's purposes and the trustee's duty of impartiality, to some or all of the beneficiaries."

Just as the thoroughbred horses were considered more important than I was, so can the special circumstances of an asset be considered more important than the requirement to diversify.

A Prudent Portfolio Is Better Than the Sum of Its Parts

We called him Zonker because he was always eating Screaming Yellow Zonkers, the candied popcorn that was so popular in the 1960s and 70s. Zonker was a mystical character who was well-known and yet completely unknown. What was really weird was that he first appeared just before the cartoon character Zonker made his debut in the Doonesbury comic strip. It was almost as if Garry Trudeau patterned his character after the *real* Zonker; a short, blond, wispy-bearded, zoned-out, pot-smoking hippie.[23]

Zonker walked slow, talked slow, and did everything else slow, except play basketball. On a basketball court, he morphed from Zonker to the Flash. He was a blur until he would plant one foot and launch himself like an Atlas rocket. You know how those rockets would seem to hover — belching smoke and fire for a few seconds after liftoff — that was Zonker; he seemed to almost stop before he rocketed upward and, at the apex of his jump, would hang weightlessly on the edge of space as the last stage separated sending the ball into the most beautiful, high-arching jump shot you ever saw.

It was rumored that Zonker had played a year for the UCLA Bruins but had quit because he didn't like the discipline of practice. I don't know if that was true, but I do know that when paired with my roommate, Doug, they were the best two-on-two basketball players in the area, and that area include a few guys who ended up in pro ball. What made them such a great pairing was that their differences complemented each other perfectly. Doug's physical inside game was the perfect complement to Zonker's outside game. If their opponents overplayed Zonker, Doug would dunk all day, and if they boxed out Doug, Zonker would pop his never-miss jumper. If they tried to play them straight up, Doug would take three steps out of the key, get the ball, and fire a guaranteed low-post turnaround bank shot. In statistical terms, the correlation coefficient between Doug and Zonker was low.

As a prudent investor, building a portfolio is all about finding investments that have relative low correlation coefficients. In a pickup basketball game if your first pick was Zonker then your second pick ought to be someone who complements him. So it is in building a portfolio; if your first pick is an investment that mirrors the S&P 500 index, then your second pick might be one that holds international stocks, similar to the MSCI EAFE, the most popular international index.

Using statistics since the inception of the MSCI EAFE in 1970, a portfolio that was 50% S&P 500 and 50% EAFE would not only have produced a higher annualized rate of return than either one alone, but it also would have done so with fewer negative quarters. Adding a third player with different skills, such as Five-Year Treasury Bonds, would result in an even higher rate of return with even fewer negative quarters.

While these relationships do not hold true over all time periods, they are consistent enough for the authors of the Uniform Prudent Investor Act to remind fiduciaries that "... investment and management decisions respecting individual assets must be evaluated not in isolation but in the context of the [investment] portfolio as a whole..." Doug and Zonker were successful because they were a good team that could complement each other's strengths and compensate for each other's weaknesses. A successful portfolio is also a good team in which each investment has a role to play. Just like Doug and Zonker, a prudent portfolio is like a team that is better than the sum of its parts.

Investors Should Avoid Sucker Pins

I calculated the distance as 195 yards and he agreed. It was perfect yardage for his four iron. While he usually pulled the club out of the bag himself, on this occasion I handed it to him. Standing off to the side of the tee, I casually glanced at the bag as he set up to the ball. To my horror I saw the "4." I went into instant panic. Looking up, I could see he was just starting his back swing. I had less than a second to make a decision. Should I yell, "stop?" Fear made the decision for me, I froze. He made perfect contact and hit a high towering shot right at the pin, but instead of landing stiff, it plugged in the top of the trap, ten yards short of the target. His expression went from disbelief to anger as he turned the club and saw the number "5" on the toe. It was definitely one of those Southwest Airlines, "Wanna get away?" commercial moments.

Over the years I have probably caddied for my brother-in-law a couple of dozen times. Jim was one of the top players on the Senior PGA Tour and being able to caddie for him was fantasy become reality. While at that moment it wasn't fun, overall, the good times far out-weighed the bad. I got to meet Arnold Palmer, Gary Player, Lee Trevino, and virtually all the other players on the Senior Tour. Trevino couldn't remember my name, but he knew I was a brother-in-law, so he called me MCI. A reference to MCI's "friends and family" calling plan, MCI was a generic name given to family members who caddied.

Caddying was fun but it was also hard work. When Jim and the other pros teed off, we caddies were usually already making our way down the fairway. By the time a pro got to his ball, the caddy should have already calculated the important yardage information, like distances to the pin, to the front of the green, and to any problem areas. The proximity of the pin to traps, water hazards, and other trouble were all important because if a pin was too close to a hazard it was known as a "sucker's pin," where a small miss could result in big trouble. In other words, a smart golfer weighs the risks and rewards of each shot to determine whether to shoot at a pin or to a safer part of the green. Even Ben Hogan, who was known as the best ball striker in the game of golf, was famous for avoiding sucker pins. Similarly, poker players call a bet where the probable return is significantly less than the amount wagered, a "sucker's bet."

Once a golfer steps onto a course, a poker player sits down at the table, or an investor gets into the market, he is exposing himself to risk. The Nobel winning economist, William Sharpe has identified two types of risk for investors (as well as golfers and poker players): compensated risk and uncompensated risk. Uncompensated risk is avoidable risk caused by concentrating in one stock or one sector of the market. According to Sharpe, this unrewarded risk can be virtually eliminated by proper diversification. Compensated risk, on the other hand, is the risk of the market as a whole and it cannot be eliminated. If an investor wants the higher expected returns of the stock market, diversification can reduce risk by eliminating uncompensated risk but it can't eliminate the compensated risk of the market which, as we have all seen, can still be quite serious.

Concentrating investments in a hot stock or sector; such as Exxon, or commodities, or even a counter-cyclical investment like gold, can be tempting. But concentration in investing is like a low probability bet in poker or a high risk shot in golf: the reward is not worth the risk. Like poker players, investors should avoid sucker bets, and, like golfers, investors should avoid sucker pins.

Fiduciaries, Like Landlords, Determine Both Suitability And Time Frame

"How do you spell *P, G and E*?" It's one of those questions that as soon as you ask it, you wish you hadn't. We had just bought a college rental for our kids and one of them, who shall remain nameless, was writing her first utility check to Pacific Gas and Electric (PG&E). We had bought the rental because we were tired of paying rent for our girls' college apartments. I remember it was not all that long after NAFTA had come out and Ross Perot had made his famous comment about "the giant sucking sound" of American jobs being pulled south of the border. I told my wife, "That sound isn't NAFTA, it's our kids sucking the money out of our wallets."

The house was in pretty good shape, considering it was a fifty-year-old tract home. The main problems were a leaky porch roof, some dry-rotted eaves, old carpet, an inefficient water heater, a backyard lawn that needed to be resodded, and windows that didn't seal tight. The windows didn't leak, but we *were* concerned because they could be pried open from the outside. With four young women living in the house, it was a safety issue that needed to be fixed relatively quickly. The other problems could be addressed within a reasonable period of time.

While reading the Uniform Prudent Investor Act, I realized that being a new landlord was not all that different from being a new trustee. The Act talks about "The Duties at Inception of Trusteeship" and says, "Within a reasonable time after accepting a trusteeship or receiving trust assets, a trustee shall review the trust assets and make and implement decisions concerning the retention and disposition of assets, in order to bring the trust portfolio into compliance with the purposes, terms, distribution requirements, and other circumstances of the trust, and with the requirements of this [Act]."

As new landlords, we needed to determine if we would patch the roof or replace it, which would in turn affect our decision about fixing the dry-rotted eaves. The carpet was worn, but it still had a few more useable years of life. We could have kept it, but we pulled it out and refinished the hardwood floors beneath. The water heater was fine when there was only one resident, but for four people it was inadequate. We could have told them to live with it, but we replaced it. Redoing the backyard was not urgent, so we put that off for six months. The windows were such a safety issue that we decided a reasonable period of time for replacing them was immediately.

Fiduciaries have to go through a similar decision-making process with their portfolio assets. In the past, a reasonable period of time for retaining or disposing of inception portfolio assets was defined as "within one year." However, the Uniform Prudent Investor Act "...retreated from this rule of thumb," saying, "No positive rule can be stated with respect to what constitutes a reasonable time for the sale or exchange of securities." The fiduciary has to make a decision on what period of time is "reasonable" based on "the totality of factors affecting the asset and the trust."

"Because it's there" might have been a good enough reason for George Mallory to climb Mount Everest, but it is *not* a good enough reason for a fiduciary to retain inception assets. When deciding whether to retain inception assets, the fiduciary needs to use the same "criteria and circumstances identified in [the] Act as bearing upon the prudence of decisions to invest and manage trust assets." The fiduciary, like the landlord, needs to determine what is suitable, and then make corrections within a reasonable period of time.

A Legacy of Loyalty

"Her name is Sarah." That was not the girl's name that my wife and I had agreed upon for our first baby, but that's the name I gave to the hospital worker. Our Sarah is the Great-great-great-great-great-granddaughter of Sarah Bradlee Fulton, who was known as the Mother of the Boston Tea Party for her participation in that event. A year and a half after the excitement of that protest on Griffin's Wharf, a more somber Sarah Bradlee Fulton stood at the window of her home in Medford town and heard "the hurrying hoof-beats of that steed, and the midnight message of Paul Revere."[24] The British were coming and it was time to choose. Joining her husband and brothers in answering that call, she grabbed bandages while they grabbed arms. The Siege of Boston had begun and, in the bloody Battle of Bunker Hill, it was Sarah who was in charge of caring for the wounded. The hill was lost but not the siege because of the courage of many a loyal patriot, not the least of whom was Sarah, who risked her life to deliver critical dispatches between Washington and spies within Boston. After the war, Washington, along with Lafayette, visited Sarah to thank her for her loyalty to the American cause.

Sarah had a choice: she could have been loyal to the British Crown or to the new nation. Investment advisors, on the other hand, have no choice about their allegiance because, as fiduciaries, they have a legal duty of loyalty to their clients. According to the Uniform Prudent Investor Act, this duty of loyalty requires fiduciaries to "...invest and manage the trust assets solely in the interest of the beneficiary." However, legislating something and *getting* it are two different things. You've all heard the expression that "you can't legislate morality." I'm not sure I agree with the context in which that statement is often used, but I do agree that morality depends on character and that Plato was right when he said that only a man who is just can be loyal. Therefore, for an unjust person, a legal duty of loyalty is no more binding than a moral duty.

Many believe that Benedict Arnold was the best general and finest leader in the Continental Army. He was smart, talented, and innovative, but he was not just, so he betrayed his country. Today, America has another smart, talented, and innovative traitor; his name is Bernie Madoff. Arnold betrayed his moral duty of loyalty to his fellow patriots for money and position; Madoff betrayed his legal duty of loyalty to his clients for his own selfish reasons.

Our country survived the betrayal of Benedict Arnold because there were thousands of loyal patriots who, like Sarah, answered the call, as Longfellow noted, "...in the hour of darkness and peril and need."[25] Our country is once again facing darkness, peril, and need, but this time it isn't the British who are coming, it's greed. Sarah was a member of the Daughters of Liberty. Today, we need investment advisors who are loyal members of the sons and daughters of responsibility. The short answer to Bernie Madoff's betrayal is oversight but, more important, it depends on investment advisors (as an industry and as individuals) stepping up to do what the SEC says we are called to do: to put clients' interests first, to act with utmost faith, to provide full and fair disclosure of all material facts, not to mislead clients, and to expose all conflicts of interest. In other words, we have a moral responsibility to fulfill our legal duty of loyalty to our clients.

My daughter Sarah is named after Sarah Bradlee Fulton to remind our family of the legacy which we have inherited and that the "fate of a nation" is now *our* responsibility. Part of that responsibility, for me, is to remember that as a husband, father, citizen, friend, and also as an investment advisor, I have a duty to leave a legacy of loyalty. So, like me, remember the legacy of Sarah and if you are a fiduciary follow her example, because you too have a duty of loyalty to the beneficiaries of your trusts, pensions, or charities.

Fiduciaries, Like Umpires, Make Decisions with Absolute Impartiality

"Strike one!" was the call, but it was a ball. The darn thing almost hit the plate. But no one yelled, "Kill the umpire!" "Strike two" *couldn't* have been a mistake — this time the ball hit the plate. But no one cried, "Fraud!" "Strike three!" Couldn't he see the ball bounce in front of the plate? I was no mighty Casey but, in the words of Ernest Thayer,[26] I had just "struck out."

I turned to the umpire in disbelief and heard him say, "Get it on the first hop." I was shocked; those weren't the rules. A strike is a pitch that crosses the plate between a batter's knees and the letters of his uniform. I dropped my bat and just stood there looking at the ump. Our coach, Mr. Thurman, came out to home plate and said something to the ump that I did not hear, picked up my bat, put his arm on my shoulders, and led me back to the dugout. I was only a ten-year-old Little Leaguer who didn't know much, but I knew I had just been cheated. I just didn't know why. Mr. Thurman knew the question without me having to ask it. He said simply, "The pitcher is the ump's kid."

According to the Umpire's Code of Ethics, "...the duty of the umpire is to act as an impartial arbitrator of [the game] and this duty carries with it an obligation to perform with accuracy, consistency, objectivity, and the highest sense of integrity."[27] The duty of a fiduciary under the Uniform Prudent Investor Act is very similar to the duty of an umpire, "If [there are] two or more beneficiaries, the [fiduciary] shall act impartially in investing and managing the [portfolio] assets, taking into account any differing interests of the beneficiaries."

What makes a good umpire is the same set of qualities that makes a good fiduciary. Just like an umpire, a fiduciary may be called upon to make decisions among competing factions. Balancing the opposing interests of income and remainder succession beneficiaries can be difficult, but making decisions among simultaneous beneficiaries with different wants and needs can be just as complicated. The skill with which these tricky situations are handled can either intensify or defuse friction among competing factions.

Correctly allocating income and principal, receipts and disbursements, taxes and tax deductions is difficult to do. To make an impartial decision is to make the decision as objectively as possible. That means knowing what the trust (or other creating document) says and using it for guidance whenever possible. If the trust is silent, then the fiduciary can use the Uniform Prudent Investor Act and its corollary, the Principal and Income Act, for guidance. Remember, as the Uniform Prudent Investor Act makes clear, the Prudent Investor Rule is considered default law; it "...may be expanded, restricted, eliminated, or otherwise altered by the provisions of a trust. A trustee is not liable to a beneficiary to the extent that the trustee acted in reasonable reliance on the provisions of the trust." So the trust is a fiduciary's first source of guidance for impartial decision making, and applicable law is second.

Major League Baseball says, "Umpires are entrusted with the integrity of the game. Those who are recruited are individuals of the highest caliber."[28] Or as former umpire Cal Hubbard put it, "Being an umpire wasn't such a tough job. You really have to understand only two things and that's knowing the rule book and maintaining discipline."[29] Being a fiduciary isn't much different; to be fair to all beneficiaries (and players), the rules must be followed, and fiduciaries (and umpires) must make decisions with absolute impartiality.

Costs Matter Because You Can't Breed or Train for Investment Performance

To the customer who asked about the cheapest way to feed his cats and dogs I said, "You could always feed the cats *to* the dogs." It was a poor attempt at humor and I deserved the reprimand that followed. At the time, I was managing a farm supply store in Chehalis, Washington and, as you can probably guess, I am not a cat person. It's not that I dislike cats, it's that I'm allergic to them. As a matter of fact, we have always had both cats and dogs. But the dogs are family, the cats are employees. Living in the country, mice get into the garage and gophers into the lawn — it's the cat's job to take care of those pests in return for room and board. Dogs, on the other hand, get a free pass even though they are pests themselves — digging up flowers, chewing drip-lines, and breaking sprinklers.

Our newest addition to this good life is a yellow Lab my wife and girls gave me a couple of Christmases ago. Aspen was a ten-month-old starter dog, which meant he'd already had enough training so he was ready to hunt. He knew the basic commands: sit, here, heel, whoa, fetch, hold, and give. When buying a Lab, you pay for both breeding and training because nature and nurture are equally important. A new, untrained Lab puppy can go for about $1000 for a male and $1200 for a female. Starter dogs run about $3000. To "finish" a dog costs $550 per month for four to six months of specialty training: either upland hunting, pheasants and quail, or duck hunting. Whether those costs are appropriate or reasonable depends on what you need the dog for.

Fiduciaries also need to weigh costs. By law they "...may only incur costs that are appropriate and reasonable in relation to the assets, the purposes of the trust, and the skills of the trustee." Real estate is a difficult asset for most trustees to manage. If a fiduciary responsible for managing real estate doesn't have training in real estate management, they should hire someone who does. They will pay extra for that skill, but it is worth it. If I wanted to do a lot of duck hunting I would pay to train Aspen in that specialty. Basically, he would need to learn to sit still until told to fetch, to "mark" (watch where a bird falls), and to take hand signals. I'd be willing to pay for this extra training because I wouldn't want to lose birds. In the same way, a fiduciary should be willing to pay extra for a person skilled in real estate to avoid losing tenants or incurring unnecessary taxes, legal fees, or other costs.

Fiduciaries are "obligated to minimize costs" and the Uniform Prudent Investor Act warns them that "...wasting beneficiaries' money is imprudent..." The Act goes on to say that when selecting mutual funds and other pooled investments, "...it is important... to make careful cost comparisons, particularly among similar products of a specific type..." So, when devising and implementing investment strategies, the default position is always "low cost."

Any deviation from low cost must be justified by the fiduciary. Superior performance would seem to be a logical justification for higher cost but, according to John Bogle, the founder of Vanguard Funds, identifying winning funds in advance is virtually impossible. Neither recent short-term nor long-term track records are good predictors of future performance, even for the best-known and best-trained fund managers. Therefore, when selecting mutual funds it is hard to justify high cost funds because, as Bogle reminds us, "Performance comes and goes, [but] costs go on forever."

There are circumstances where fiduciaries can justify higher costs, like when a specialty skill in real estate is needed. However, making the case for higher cost mutual funds is more difficult because, unlike a good dog, there is virtually no evidence that fund managers can be bred or trained to improve performance.

Fiduciaries, Like Backpackers, Focus on Efficiency and Value

When I was hitchhiking around the country in the early 1970s, the most likely person to pick me up was a woman in her 40's or 50's. And the first words out of her mouth were always, "You know, I have a son about your age."

With a Kelty backpack, a North Face sleeping bag, some homemade trail mix and a bottle of Dr. Bronner's Magic Peppermint Oil Soap©, I had everything I needed for hiking in the wilderness or hitching across the country. The peppermint soap was my most efficient item — I used it for everything: washing dishes, clothes, hair, body, and even as tooth paste. In the woods I would wet my hair and then lather up all over with the liquid soap before a quick dip in a stream. And I *do* mean quick. On the road, instead of bathing in the woods I used a gas station restroom. The procedure started the same by wetting my hair and lathering up, but instead of jumping into a stream, I used a coffee can to dump the water from the sink over my body. It was best to do this about 2:00 in the morning, that way if I got interrupted it was usually by someone from the bar crowd who was so drunk he thought he was seeing things.

Whether I was hitchhiking or backpacking, I had to learn to be very efficient since everything I needed to sustain myself had to fit either *in* or *on* my pack. Tax efficiency is just as important for the survival of a fiduciary's portfolios as packing efficiency was for my personal survival. According to the Uniform Prudent Investor Act, "Among circumstances that a trustee shall consider in investing and managing trust assets are... the expected tax consequences of investment decisions or strategies..." The Act goes on to mention a number of tax situations that should be carefully considered. For one, "...trust beneficiaries are in general best served by an investment strategy that minimizes the taxation incident to portfolio turnover." As Warren Buffett puts it, this "...is not a tax on capital gains, it's a tax on transactions. High turnover creates recognition of capital gains, which can be taxed at ordinary income rates if the security is held for less than one year." Buffett is very adamant that frequent trading is neither tax-efficient, because of the taxes recognized, nor cost-effective, because of the trading cost incurred. Because of their low turnover in addition to their minimal fees, index mutual funds would appear to be an excellent investment choice for most fiduciaries. For these reasons, Buffett says "Most investors, both institutional and individual, will find that the best way to own common stocks is through an index fund... Those following this path are sure to beat the net results (after fees, [taxes] and expenses) delivered by the great majority of investment professionals."

The Act also mentions that it is "exceptionally" important to preserve the stepped-up basis on death for low-basis assets, to consider buying tax-free bonds in charitable trusts because of the pass-through of taxes to the beneficiary, and to even consider not diversifying a block of low-basis securities for "tax-sensitive trusts."

Tax-efficiency is prominently mentioned in the Uniform Prudent Investor Act and fiduciaries should be very careful to consider the effect of taxes on the portfolios they manage. This is especially important "When tax considerations affect beneficiaries differently, the trustee's duty of impartiality requires attention to the competing interests of each of them." As a backpacker, I needed to focus on the things that were efficient and added significant value. Dr. Bronner's Magic Peppermint Oil Soap was as important to me as tax efficiency is to a fiduciary.

Since Decisions Can't Be Made In Hindsight, Fiduciaries Aren't Judged In Hindsight

"At least you're half of rich and famous." That statement by my wife was meant to encourage me, but it felt more like sarcasm. It was the year 2000. I had just spent almost four years writing a program that performed all the calculations for the proposed minimum required distribution laws, and now the IRS had just changed the rules after fifteen years, making my years of work worthless.

In the mid-nineties I saw that the Baby Boomers had trillions of dollars in retirement plans and, while everyone else was trying to figure out how to get more money *into* those plans, I realized that it wouldn't be long before the Boomers would need help in getting the money *out*. I started studying the situation and discovered the biggest problem was navigating the incredibly complex minimum required distribution laws. Since there were not many articles on the subject, I turned to the source and read the law and the related proposed regulations.

The one book on minimum required distributions was *Life and Death Planning for Retirement Benefits*. It was, and still is, the bible for retirement distribution planning. Reading the book, I noticed a couple of tables with incorrect numbers so I called the author, Natalie Choate, and not so tactfully said, "Nice book, but your numbers are wrong." Ah, the arrogance of ignorance. She was gracious to this bumbling idiot who had somehow stumbled on a couple of errors and asked me how I caught them. I told her, "With some computer software." She replied, "There *isn't* any software that would catch those problems." Well there was, and I had written it. That's when I realized that I really had something special. It was 1996 and I started my four-year quest to improve, test, and make my software user-friendly.

Looking at the demographics, the difficulty of understanding the law, and the severe consequences of poor decisions, it looked like a very prudent thing for me to spend the time and money developing the program. It would be worth a fortune because virtually every CPA and tax attorney would need a copy. Upon completion of the program, I received rave reviews from some national magazines and got a plug for it in Natalie's book as well as another widely read book on distributions by Ed Slott. The IRS contacted me about obtaining a license and I signed an agreement with a software company to distribute it. It looked like I had made the right decision and things were about to pay off. And that's when I got the news that instantly took me from the "thrill of victory" to "the agony of defeat."[30]

I ended up wasting four years developing something that became obsolete five minutes after it was completed. As it turned out, developing the software was *not* the right thing to do, but was it a prudent thing to do? Based on the facts and circumstances at the time, it *was* a prudent decision. According to the Uniform Prudent Investor Act this is how fiduciaries are to be judged. As the Act points out, "Not every investment or management decision will turn out in the light of hindsight to have been successful. Hindsight is not the relevant standard. In the language of law and economics, the standard is *ex ante*, not *ex post*."

A friend of mine likes to kid me by saying, "It's a good thing you're good because you sure as heck aren't lucky." I don't know if that is true, but I *do* know that if you learn your skill well and consistently apply prudent principles, you will increase your odds of success. As a fiduciary, you are called to follow a prudent process because that is what is best for your beneficiary and that is the standard by which you will be judged. In hindsight, writing the software was the wrong thing to do but, just like me, fiduciaries have to make decisions without the benefit of hindsight. Since decisions can't be made in hindsight, fiduciaries aren't judged in hindsight either.

A Prudent Expert, Unlike A Girlfriend, Can Lessen Your Liability

"You are the worst writer I have ever seen in the UC system." Those were the encouraging words of my "bonehead English" class professor who flunked me five times (and I earned every one of those F's.) Passing remedial English was a pre-requisite for literacy-challenged students before they could take the required English general education courses. It's an understatement to say that English was difficult for me. I scored close to the 800 points maximum on the math section of the SAT test and virtually zero on the English portion.

Numbers make sense to me: two plus two always equals four, but "'i' before 'e' except after 'c'" is some kind of w**ei**rd, for**ei**gn, unsc**ie**ntific rule. Compound interest and you get rich, but compound sentences don't make sense. The only thing worse than English was Spanish; I couldn't even figure out my *own* language and they wanted me to pass a foreign language. I actually petitioned the college to have my bonehead English count for my foreign language requirement. And why not? It was a foreign language to me and I had taken more than the required four quarters. After flunking out of French and Italian as well as Spanish, the university finally waived my foreign language requirement. The only good thing about the whole ordeal was that when I went to Europe, I could ask for a beer and the bathroom in four languages.

With all my language class problems, I didn't have enough time to do my other schoolwork, so I had to learn the art of delegation. While my buddies were choosing girlfriends based on their looks, I was looking for someone who could write (and type) term papers. I may have been the only guy in the history of college dating who was accused by his girlfriends of only wanting them for their minds.

I delegated term papers out of the recognition that I was not competent enough to write them myself. However, it took an additional twenty years before trust and fiduciary law came around to this point of view. In recognition of the complexity of modern life and the sophistication of modern investment products, the law forbidding fiduciaries to delegate investment and management functions was reversed in 1992 with the *Restatement (Third) of Trusts (Prudent Investor Rule)* and later by the Uniform Prudent Investor Act, which incorporated those changes.

The law now says, "A trustee has a duty personally to perform the responsibilities of trusteeship except as a prudent person might delegate those responsibilities to others..." It goes on to say that a fiduciary must be prudent in determining "...whether, to whom, and in what manner to delegate..." and then to follow up by prudently monitoring the activities of the agents chosen.

The Uniform Prudent Investor Act, Employee Retirement Income Security Act, and the Uniform Prudent Management of Institutional Funds Act all allow fiduciaries of private trusts, pensions, and charitable organizations to delegate investment decisions to investment advisors and other prudent experts. If the fiduciary is prudent in the selection and monitoring of an investment advisor who is willing and able to accept discretion, then the fiduciary is not liable to the beneficiaries of the trust, pension, or charity for the decisions or actions of the investment advisors to whom the investment function was delegated. In other words, the prudent delegation of investment decision making can significantly reduce the personal liability of the fiduciary.

While delegating the writing of term papers to girlfriends probably wasn't prudent, the delegation of investment decisions to an investment advisor *is* prudent because, unlike a girlfriend, a prudent expert can lessen your liability.

Section 5

Making Choices: Process vs. Predictions, Brokers vs. Investment Advisors, Active vs. Passive Investing, Bond Returns vs. Bond Stability, and What Works vs. What Sells

"Those who have knowledge, don't predict.
Those who predict, don't have knowledge."
- Lao Tzu

Because of the uncertainty of life, wise choices are based on prudent decisions, not attempts to predict the future. Since, as a fiduciary, it is your duty to put the "best interest" of your beneficiaries first, it is important to know what is prudent and what is not. Among the decisions you will need to make are choosing between a broker or an investment advisor, active or passive management, volatile or stable bonds, and what works or what sells.

Fiduciaries Handle Uncertainty by Following a Prudent Process

"What's so funny?" the bank teller asked. She could tell I was amused but she didn't know why. I said "Look around. This is bank robber heaven. Everyone in the bank is wearing a mask, including you." We were all wearing masks because we were concerned about the effect of breathing volcanic ash. It was 1980 and Mount St. Helens had recently erupted just forty miles from our little town of Chehalis, WA. In the hours after the eruption, it was pitch black and eerily quiet as what looked like gray talcum power gently drifted to the ground. When the unnatural storm finally cleared, the ground was covered with an inch of ash and the top quarter of the mountain that had always loomed over my neighbor's house was gone.

Before the eruption there was a whole lot of uncertainty about what was going to happen, and afterwards there was a whole lot of uncertainty about what to do. The ash was about 65% silica and was very abrasive. It was so fine it would get into everything and so gritty that it would wear out anything with moving parts. The local farmers had all kinds of problems, especially with their hay cutting equipment which was exposed to the ash covered crops. To protect their engines, the state police mounted auxiliary air filters on the fronts of their cars. I just parked my new car in the garage and didn't drive it. I don't know if it was the right thing to do, but it was a prudent choice under the circumstances.

Investing also involves a whole lot of uncertainty, and investor attempts to reduce this uncertainty usually involves some kind of forecasting. While forecasting volcanic eruptions has become more accurate with modern equipment, economic forecasting has not improved with technology. It is true that far more information is available these days but, because it is so widely distributed, it is harder than ever to find hidden treasures. In addition, markets are not only affected by facts, but also by investors' emotional responses to real or perceived facts. These emotional responses cause sudden swings in markets that are impossible to predict and, therefore, impossible to time. Finally, there is the cruelty of mathematics — losses have a bigger impact than gains — so you have to be right significantly more often than you are wrong in order to beat markets.

Because prudence recognizes the limitations of forecasting, it relies on following the right *process* instead of trying to guess the right *choice*. Just as scientists use the scientific method as a process for experimentation, fiduciaries use the "prudent process", outlined in the Uniform Prudent Investor Act, as their guide for making investment decisions. According to the Act, a prudent process begins with defining risk and return objectives that are reasonably suited to the beneficiary's situation. An investment strategy can then be established that considers the purposes, terms, distribution requirements, and other circumstances of the investor. Implementation of this strategy requires the exercise of reasonable care, skill, and caution. It also requires the knowledge of basic economic concepts which mandate that individual assets are evaluated in the context of the investment portfolio as a whole, that the portfolio is well diversified, and that cost and taxes are kept low.

The uncertainty surrounding Mount St. Helens caused a lot of fear among local residents. Volcanic eruptions in markets cause fear among investors as well. However, fiduciaries should not attempt to reduce the fear caused by uncertainty by trying to forecast markets. Uncertainty in nature, as well as in markets, is best handled by following a prudent process.

I Can Only Claim It Is 100% Pure If It Really Is 100% Pure

"Let those eastern bastards freeze in the dark." That sign was held up by an Edmonton Eskimo fan at the 1973 Grey Cup game held in Toronto. What upset the western Canadians was that they had the natural resources but the easterners had the votes. The result of this political mismatch was the National Energy Policy, which forced the western provinces to sell their oil to the eastern provinces at a rate substantially below the world market price. At the time of the Grey Cup, I was working in Toronto, driving a truck for a honey packaging plant. I'd made the job contact while working for a beekeeper north of Edmonton, so I understood how the westerners felt, which caused me to feel a little guilty for enjoying the cheap fuel back east.

Enjoying the cheap gas, however, wasn't the only thing I felt guilty about. Occasionally, when I had no deliveries, I would work on the production line in the honey packaging plant. What bothered me was there was one production line but two different labels: our regular one and an "All Natural" one. When I checked the prices, the "All Natural" honey sold for twice as much, even though the only difference was the label. I was also bothered by the fact that both labels said "100% Canadian," when I knew that over half of the honey was cheaper Argentine honey. My boss explained that the law allowed the hundred percent claim if it was at least fifty-percent Canadian, "and the jars were made in Canada."

Years later, working for a brokerage company, I was again uncomfortable with the business practices of my employer which, while legal and common, did not require them to provide clients with the best products at the best price. When looking into the different investment alternatives offered by my firm, I was shocked to find how difficult it was to determine the true costs. Certain fees such as 12(b)-1 fees, annuity costs, and distribution fees were disclosed, but they were also somewhat obscure, and it was impossible to determine *who* was getting *what*. When I asked about one such charge, a mutual fund company representative hesitated and then said, "You'd better talk to your firm about that."

The real shocker was to find out that there were some fees that were completely hidden. Trading costs and soft dollar fees are not disclosed anywhere and are only known by the investment fund managers and the brokerage firm that clears their trades. The brokerage industry has gotten so good at hiding fees that the US Government Accountability Office (GAO) told Congress in 2006 that the Department of Labor (DOL) could not do their job of overseeing investment costs in pension plans because it "...lacks the information it needs to provide effective oversight." If brokerage fees are so confusing that even the DOL and GAO can't figure them out, what chance do we have?

When I asked my boss about it he said, "It's none of your damn business, it's your business to sell." And you know the sad thing? He was right. As a registered representative I was an employee and legally required to put the interests of my firm above the best interest of my client. Advice was considered legally "suitable" even if I knew it wasn't the *best* advice.

Now, as a Registered Investment Advisor, I am held to a fiduciary standard and I am legally required to provide my clients my best advice. I owe a fiduciary duty to my clients, and to them alone, because, as an Investment Advisor, I have no broker dealer. My honey company boss could make his 100% claim because, like my broker dealer boss, he was held to a suitability standard. But as a fiduciary, I can only claim it is 100% pure if it really is 100% pure.

The Magic Word is Prudence

My dad was very reluctant to buy a television; he called it the "idiot box." However, once we got a TV in the late 1950s, he got hooked on two shows: *You Bet Your Life* with Groucho Marx and the *Friday Night Fights*. The one thing I remember about Groucho Marx was the "magic word" (he pronounced it "woid"). Groucho would tell each contestant, "Say the magic word and win a prize." Friday Night Fights began with the ring announcer introducing the fighters with great fanfare, "In this corner weighing..." It was at this point that Dad and I would choose sides; I would bet on one fighter and Dad would place his bet on the other fighter. It wasn't a financial bet, just bragging rights.

Fiduciaries who are responsible for investment portfolios place bets as well, but they are real financial bets. The problem is that too many fiduciaries are placing bets on the wrong fighter. The fighter I mean is otherwise known as an "active" investment manager, a real underdog with steep odds stacked against him. An active manager is a losing fighter. A winning fighter is a "passive" investment manager, the clear favorite with steep odds stacked in his favor. Many fiduciaries (as well as many investors) end up choosing the wrong fighter because they are confused about their records and because they don't know the magic word: prudence.

Active investment managers sell themselves as very bright people (most, in fact, are) with the ability to "beat the market" by picking outperforming stocks and by timing the ups and downs of stock market cycles. Passive investment managers, on the other hand, don't attempt to beat the market; they just want to match the market by investing in index funds that take advantage of the excess returns stocks have historically earned. Active managers accuse passive managers of settling for average, while passive managers decry active management as a fool's game.

Although I am a proponent of passive investing, that doesn't mean I believe that an active manager can't occasionally outperform a passive strategy (although identifying that manager in advance is next to impossible). But that is the wisdom of prudence. Prudence doesn't require right results because right results assume an ability to foresee the future. Instead, it obligates a fiduciary investor to follow the "right process." This switch in the focus of prudence from *results* to *process* was laid down by the Uniform Prudent Investor Act which undertook the task of incorporating the principles of Modern Portfolio Theory into the investment conduct of fiduciaries. As the Prefatory Note to the Uniform Prudent Investor Act states, the purpose of the Act was "...to update trust investment law in recognition of the alterations that have occurred in investment practice. These changes have occurred under the influence of a large and broadly accepted body of empirical and theoretical knowledge about the behavior of capital markets, often described as 'Modern Portfolio Theory.'"[31] (The Uniform Prudent Management of Institutional Funds Act now applies these updated "rules on investment decision making ... to charities organized as nonprofit corporations."[32])

One of the basic assumptions of Modern Portfolio Theory is that returns on stocks (and other securities) are random and, therefore, unknowable. Another is that investors are risk-averse; that is, given two investments with the same expected return, an investor will chose the one with the lower risk. The solution to overcoming the inherent problem of randomness in securities returns and the risk aversion of investors is diversification. Diversification is not achieved by selecting great numbers of investments or — as strange as it may seem — by attempting to select investments with the highest expected returns. Rather, truly efficient and effective diversification occurs when a number of investments, which are significantly different from one another, are selected for a portfolio.

Over the years, economists and other academicians have added to the body of knowledge underlying Modern Portfolio Theory by identifying factors that enhance portfolio returns and those that detract from returns. Researchers have discovered that returns are enhanced not only by a portfolio's percentage allocation to stocks, but also by portfolio weighting toward small stocks and value stocks. Small and value stocks enhance returns because of their higher expected return and their lower correlation to the overall market. Lower correlation is just another way of saying these stocks act differently from other stocks to market events. Research has also shown that the slow erosion of portfolio values caused by the effects of costs and taxes can be as devastating to portfolio values as the volatility of sudden market swings.

Modern Portfolio Theory is the reason why the Uniform Prudent Investor Act states that, when implementing an investment strategy, a prudent process requires the exercise of reasonable care, skill, and caution and the duty "to diversify," "to minimize costs," and to "consider... tax consequences." While these requirements would seem to strongly favor the use of passive investing, the authors of the *Restatement (Third) of Trusts (Prudent Investor Rule)* — the forebear of the Uniform Prudent Investor Act and the source of its interpretation — made every effort to avoid the suggestion that active investing was impermissible. While seemingly contradictory, this reluctance to exclude active investing is understandable, given that one of the objectives of modern prudent fiduciary investment precepts was to avoid declaring any type of investment as "inherently imprudent" or, conversely, creating "legal lists of approved trust investments."[33]

The Restatement, therefore, allows departures from what is normally considered a prudent process. Any such departure is justifiable if it can be shown that there is "...a realistically evaluated prospect of enhanced return."[34] This Restatement commentary is confusing since it seems to switch prudence back to results instead of process. After all, active investing, by its very nature, entails some kind of investment concentration (the very opposite of broad diversification which underlies Modern Portfolio Theory) in an attempt to increase returns, and it usually incurs extra costs and taxes that are the consequence of research expenses and portfolio turnover.

However, given the reluctance of the authors of the Restatement to exclude active investing, and considering that when the Restatement and the Uniform Prudent Investor Act were first promulgated in the early 1990s, Peter Lynch had just resigned after a phenomenal run as the manager of Fidelity Magellan, it probably seemed logical, at the time, that some brilliant active managers had a "realistically evaluated prospect of enhanced return" — that is, a chance of beating the market. A decade and a half later, it's time to revisit this assumption. Why? Because if we compare the records of the two fighters — an active manager and a passive manager — it's rather clear that the passive manager has won, making that approach the one to be followed by prudent fiduciaries. The active manager, on the other hand, is free to carry on his speculative ways but he cannot use a process under modern prudent fiduciary investing as a defense for his investment conduct.

The track record of the active investing icon, Peter Lynch, is as good a place as any to begin a comparison of active investing and passive investing. Lynch was named the manager of Fidelity Magellan, a small obscure mutual fund, in 1977. By the time he left in 1990, he had generated a total return of 2,475%, which crushed the 518% return of the S&P 500 index over the same period; he had grown Magellan's assets from $18 million to $14 billion, making that fund the best-known name in active investing.

Was Lynch's performance due to skill or luck? No one knows for sure because a 13-year track record is not enough time to statistically prove for sure that a manager is skillful. In fact, it takes over 30 years of data to say, with statistical certainty, that stocks outperform Treasury bills even though stocks *have* historically outperformed Treasury bills by almost 3 to 1. According to Ted Aronson of the investment firm Aronson and Partners, "It takes between 20 and 80 years of monitoring performance to statistically prove that a money manager is skillful rather than lucky — which is a lot more than most people have in mind when they say 'long term'."[35]

Even more sobering is the little-known fact that virtually no one actually received the returns posted by Magellan during Lynch's tenure. During the first five years of his run, Lynch outperformed the S&P 500 index by about 25% per year, but in his last eight years that outperformance had shrunk to about 3% per year. By 1977 though, Magellan had only 9,227 shareholders and, by the end of his hottest two-year period in 1980, that number had dropped to 6,791. In an interview after his retirement, Lynch acknowledged this problem by saying, "Magellan is up 26-fold in 13 years. But no one was in it 13 years ago. In 10 years, it is up nine or 10-fold. But no one was in it 10 years ago."[36] As W. Scott

Simon points out in his book, *Index Mutual Funds: Profiting from an Investment Revolution*, "Even when investors are able to identify a fabulous record and attempt to get a piece of it, the winning mutual fund has usually already peaked in performance... This unceasing flow of money directed at Magellan in the hope that Lynch would duplicate the excellence of his past (which turned out to be largely fruitless), coincided with the period when Lynch was only 4-3 against the market."[37]

A more recent investment icon, Bill Miller, who is the manager of the Legg Mason Value Trust, outperformed the S&P 500 index for 15 straight years from 1991 through 2005. Unlike Lynch, Miller came to the attention of investors much more quickly while he was still "hot." By the end of the 1990s, Morningstar had chosen Miller as the "Fund Manager of the Decade" after naming him the "Fund Manager of the Year" the previous year. Money magazine called him, "The Greatest Money Manager of the 1990s." As late as 2005, both Business Week and The Wall Street Journal selected him for their highest awards as one of the nation's exceptional mutual fund managers. While Lynch invested in well over 1,000 stocks in Magellan, Miller concentrated his holdings in only a limited number of stocks; a check with Morningstar revealed recently that he held only 39 securities.

Miller apparently believes that he has the ability to pick winners, so there's no reason to diversify — just pick the best and sit back and rake in the money. Miller's recent picks, unfortunately, have been financial stocks such as Bear Stearns, Merrill Lynch, Citigroup and Countrywide. Maybe his college major should have been in economics instead of philosophy; he might have realized the big risks he was taking by concentrating in a limited number of stocks in an even more limited number of market sectors. Miller's shareholders may not be too happy with a philosophical explanation for what, in the words of Morningstar, "...has changed a once superior long-term return into a subpar one... its 10-year return is among the very worst of the 300 large-blend funds that have been around that long."[38] The Massachusetts state pension fund has learned its lesson and fired Miller along with a number of other active managers, and replaced them with managers following a more passive investment style. Miller, on the other hand, still refused to admit his mistakes and gambled that the credit crunch would soon be ending. His gamble: placing a huge bet on Freddie Mac. That is a sucker's bet — whether or not it would have turned out to be the right one — a kind of bet that a prudent fiduciary should never make.

Looking at the track records of the two best active mutual fund managers, it would be difficult to say if their performances were due to skill or to luck, because neither one could sustain his performance; Lynch cooled off and Miller crashed. I know of no way, in the present, to choose investment managers with "...a realistically evaluated prospect of enhanced return[s]." Going forward, it should be even *more* difficult, according to a study recently highlighted in The New York Times. The study, "False Discoveries in Mutual Fund Performance: Measuring Luck in Estimating Alphas," used a statistical test known as the "False Discovery Rate" to account for luck when determining the number of funds with truly positive (or negative) performances. The researchers concluded that it used to be that a small percentage of active investment managers could beat the market, but today that number is "...statistically indistinguishable from zero."[39] That "...doesn't mean that no mutual funds have beaten the market in recent years [but] the 'number that have beaten the market over their entire histories is so small that the False Discovery Rate test can't eliminate the possibility that the few that did were merely false positives'—just lucky, in other words."[40]

For the prudent fiduciary, this means that, in the past, there was a very small possibility of choosing a fund with a realistic chance of beating the market. Today that chance is statistically (and, therefore, realistically) zero. With no realistic defense for active investing remaining, it would be imprudent for a fiduciary to place any bets on this losing fighter. That's especially true since betting on the winning fighter, passive investing, lessens liability by allowing the fiduciary to utter the magic word: prudence.

Bonds Are For Stability, Not Return

In early July of 1953, the Rattlesnake Fire broke out in the narrow and brush-choked Grindstone Canyon on the Mendocino National Forest. Along with the regular fire-fighters, a group of twenty-five volunteers from the nearby New Tribes Missions training facility had been called upon to battle the blaze. After a long day, and with the fire seemingly under control, the weary volunteer firefighters sat down to have a quick boxed-meal before walking out of the canyon. For fifteen of the twenty-five missionaries, it was to be their last supper.

Fifty years later I stood in that same canyon with my Dad, observing the dedication of a memorial to those fallen men. Following tearful remembrances, an inexperienced public information officer was struggling to explain the circumstances that had caused the tragedy. Dad, now in his nineties, shuffled forward causing a murmur as the veteran firefighters turned and explained to those nearby them that this old man now standing before them was an iconic fire boss and the person who pioneered the use of fire retardant dropping airplanes. Using his cane as a pointer and the canyon as his visual aid, he proceeded to explain how topography, vegetation, and wind currents transformed a tranquil setting into a sudden tragedy.

Fires are a natural and necessary way to clear excess underbrush and rejuvenate forests. Financial markets, too, have natural cycles where excess growth is reduced by periods of decline, contraction, or even recessions. But catastrophic fires, as well as catastrophic market declines, can cause damage that may take years to recover from. One way of eliminating this volatility in portfolios would be to eliminate all investments in stocks. Unfortunately, this would be as unhealthy for most portfolios as it would be to remove all vegetation from a mountain just to prevent forest fires. A deforested hillside would be exposed to significant soil erosion and a portfolio devoid of stocks would experience the constant erosion of inflation.

Healthy forest management practices reduce volatile fuel loads to an acceptable level by the use of firebreaks, control burns, and other methods of removing excess vegetation. Healthy portfolio management practices reduce volatility by diversification. But diversification alone can't remove enough volatility for all but the bravest (or maybe craziest) investors, so we add bonds to our portfolios for increased stability. However, not all bonds reduce volatility.

Bond quality, along with term length, determines the volatility of bonds; as the quality declines returns increase, but so does risk. In periods of severe economic distress the flight to quality often causes the value of all but the highest quality bonds to fall. In 2008, medium quality bonds were down about 12%, junk bonds dropped more than 25%, and the supposedly safe adjustable-rate bank loans were off by more than 30%. Only the highest quality corporate bonds, along with US Government bonds, increased in value that year.

Dad knew that you can't eliminate fires from forests and I know you can't eliminate risk from portfolios, but with good management practices, you can reduce the losses. Dad used firebreaks to keep wildfires under control and we use bonds to keep portfolio volatility under control. But many bond and fixed-income managers have delivered unexpectedly large losses at precisely the time when stability was most needed because they did not understand the function of bonds in a portfolio. We always keep our bonds high in quality and short in maturity, because we know bonds are for stability, not return.

What Works, Not What Sells

Have you ever artificially inseminated a queen bee? I did when I worked for Mr. Clarence. Clarence was actually his first name, but somehow out of a combination of respect and affection he got the nickname "Mr. Clarence." Mr. Clarence was a commercial beekeeper who had a passion for finding better ways of doing things, which is why he had us artificially inseminating bees. At this point, if you are like most people, you must be asking yourself, "How?" Well, it involves a microscope and some miniature equipment that sort of resembles a cross between Frankenstein's laboratory and a horse stud barn. While I still smile remembering some of the jokes, what Mr. Clarence helped to pioneer was no joke; especially now when Colony Collapse Disorder is jeopardizing the one-third of our nation's food supply that is dependent upon bee pollination. If the honeybee is to be saved (and thus our food supply), it may be because of genetic research and selective breeding made possible by artificially inseminating queen bees.

Dr. Harry Laidlaw, professor of entomology at the University of California, Davis, was the man who developed artificial insemination of bees, but his significance in the field of bee genetics was much greater than that. As one of his colleagues put it, "All of us who have made our careers studying the genetics of honey bees stand on the shoulders of Harry Laidlaw." Dr. Laidlaw and Mr. Clarence worked closely with each other, sharing ideas and techniques on bee breeding and queen rearing. It was Dr. Laidlaw who taught Mr. Clarence, along with a few of his employees, including myself, how to instrumentally inseminate queen bees.

Mr. Clarence, the commercial beekeeper, and Dr. Laidlaw, the college professor, collaborated because they were both motivated by the desire to create healthier and more productive bees. By applying academic research to real world situations, they were able to develop stronger colonies for pollinating crops and for producing honey. Mr. Clarence wasn't the only beekeeper whose main business was selling queen bees, but his commitment to breeding and genetics was unusual. While the other beekeepers were concentrating on selling more queens, Mr. Clarence was determined to find ways to breed better queens.

As a financial advisor, I have noticed a similar situation among investment product providers. Much of the industry seems to be focused on the quantity of sales instead of the quality of the product. The result is that what they are selling isn't always in the best interest of the investor. A good example of this is equity index annuities: a very complicated product that is often touted as the perfect investment, one that gets the gains of the stock market without the losses. In other words, what is being sold is the illusion of high returns with no risks. What the investor often gets is a product with high fees and a long surrender period that seems to be designed more for the benefit of the investment company than for the investor.

However, there are product providers who, like Mr. Clarence, have a passion for figuring out what works. These firms are committed to identifying and applying the factors that drive performance for their client, not just the factors that drive their own bottom line. As a fiduciary, it is your job to sort through the different mutual funds, annuities, managed accounts, and other investments to find these good product providers among the bad, and the ugly. At the time, I never noticed how different Mr. Clarence's bee business was and how important that difference was for the success of his clients, the health of the industry, and the greater good of our society. To find good investment products, you need to look for companies that have the same attitude that made Mr. Clarence different: a passion for figuring out what works, not what sells.

Section 6

Do It! Don't Do It!: Avoiding Emotional Responses to Markets

"Knowing is not enough; we must apply.
Willing is not enough; we must do."
- Johann Wolfgang von Goethe

Knowing isn't enough because we are hardwired
to do dumb things when it comes to money.
Therefore, as a fiduciary, you need the
courage to do the right things
and the discipline not to do the wrong things.

Prudent Investors, Like Disciplined Runners, Just Do It

Nike might have trademarked "Just Do It®" in 1992, but I heard Jim Ryan, the former world record holder in the mile, utter that phrase twenty years earlier. At the time, he was preparing for the 1972 Olympics and he occasionally did some of his workouts on our track. On one such occasion, someone asked him how he found time to workout and he said, "Every day there are a half dozen good reasons why you should skip your workout, but you have to ignore them and just do it."

I ran track at UC Santa Barbara and I have kept up a daily workout routine ever since. I was probably the worst distance runner to ever make the track team. My claim to fame was a photo in the local paper showing me just being edged out at the tape by Dennis Savage, who had run internationally for the US Track Team. The caption said, "Savage Edges Out Unknown Santa Barbara Runner." What the caption *didn't* say was I still had a lap to go. I won the green jock award for that one. It was a jock strap that was dyed green and the distance runner who did the dumbest thing had to wear the darn thing as a headband during the next week's workouts.

They called us distance runners the "Animals" because of the brutal distances we ran, over a hundred miles a week during the off season. In season, we usually ran a little less because we did interval work on the track a couple of times a week to build up speed and recovery. A typical interval workout might be 40 quarters (once around the track) with a one-ten (110 yard) jog in between. Our daily workouts were posted on a chalkboard just inside the locker room. Each day I looked at the workout, and each day I had to resist the urge to quit.

Today, as an investment advisor I look at a different chalkboard — actually a webpage that has the returns for the different security markets posted on it. Each day for the last 18 months, I have looked at that webpage and, each day, I have had to resist the urge to quit.* Not only do I hear that little inner-voice screaming "stop!" but I also see headlines proclaiming that everything I have learned and believe about investing is dead. Indexing is dead. Buy and hold is dead. Stock investing is dead. Global investing is dead. Passive investing is dead. Even diversification is dead. The death knell has been sounded because broad diversification within and across asset classes has not worked in the short run and all the equity markets, most of the commodities, and many of the bond markets have dropped significantly. My confidence is shaken as doubt joins fear in shouting "It really *is* different this time."

But *is it* really different? I don't think so. The decline is deeper and longer, but I don't think the rules have really changed. Instead of being a time to quit, it's time to persevere, "...to persist in an undertaking and to maintain a purpose in spite of difficulty, obstacles, or discouragement."[41] As a runner, when I felt like quitting, my fellow runners would encourage me to take one more step. As an advisor and fellow investor, I want to encourage *you* to take one more step. As you take that step, remember we are trying to *get* market returns, not beat them. As you take that next step, remember that markets are volatile enough without us making them even more volatile by trying to out-guess them. As you continue to put one foot in front of the other, remember to persevere when you hear that little voice of doubt and fear.

Every day the news gives us a whole lot of very good reasons why we should get out of the market, but you need to ignore them. Like disciplined runners, prudent investors "just do it."

**This was written as a newsletter in February of 2009 before the market recovery.*

If It Feels Right, Don't Do It

In a 1998 speech during the height of the dot-com bubble, Alan Greenspan said "...just as a bull stock market feels unending and secure as an economy and stock market move forward, so it can feel when markets contract that recovery is inconceivable. Both, of course, are wrong. But because of the difficulty imagining a turnabout when such emotions take hold, periods of euphoria or distress tend to feed on themselves."

This triumph of emotion over reason may actually be biological. Neuroscience tells us that the brain activity of a person experiencing financial gains is indistinguishable from the activity of someone high on cocaine and that the region of the brain that processes financial losses is the same region that processes mortal danger. Neurological research has also confirmed what Greenspan observed, that we believe current circumstances will continue forever because our brains have seen a series of either gains or losses and have automatically (and subconsciously) accepted the notion that this current pattern will be repeated. When the pattern is broken, our brains respond with alarm. But broken patterns are a common — and often necessary — part of the cycles we find in nature, history, science, and even in our own bodies.[42]

Some cycles, like planetary orbits, are consistent and predictable, while others, such as financial market cycles, are inconsistent and full of random elements. However, even with their randomness, market cycles *do* have discernable patterns: rising, peaking, falling, and bottoming. When markets rise, we go from optimism to euphoria. The overwhelming urge at this point is to pour money into the market and concentrate it in the hottest sectors. Near the peak of the cycle we are full of confidence and know we are doing the right thing. Once markets start falling, our optimism turns to anxiety and we begin questioning our decisions. Our confidence is shaken, but we hold on by reminding ourselves to think long-term. Finally, as the downturn accelerates and losses mount, fear and panic convince us that we are dreadfully wrong and we need to get out.[43]

Our emotional responses to different market cycle stages are normal. It's reacting to these emotions that creates the problem. Morningstar's Investor Returns tool (which compares the returns investors actually earned to the returns their mutual funds earned) shows that investors significantly under-perform their funds because they move money *in* after gains and *out* after losses. They buy high and sell low, understandable but costly. According to Dalbar Inc., the Boston based investment research firm, the average investor loses two-thirds of his or her potential return due to poor decisions. They calculated that between 1986 and 2005, an S&P 500 index fund earned almost 12%, but the average mutual fund investor earned less than 4%. The average professional didn't do much better. According to Anders Ericsson, who *Time* magazine called the world's leading expert on experts, experienced professional investors "...are barely better than novices."

So, if you can't trust your feelings and you can't trust the experts, who *do* you trust? You trust the things that consistently make a difference: you buy index funds, you broadly diversify across different asset classes, you keep costs low, and you decide to stay the course when things look hopeless. And how do you stay the course? That's easy, "If it feels right, don't do it!"

Section 7

You First: Stories About My Heroes

If I... can fathom all mysteries and all knowledge...
but have not love, I am nothing.
If I give all I possess to the poor,
but have not love, I gain nothing.
1 Corinthian 13:2, 3

As a fiduciary, you are responsible for knowing your duties and for doing your duties.
Do that and you will protect yourself from legal liability. However, to me life is much more than fulfilling the minimum standards to get by.
Following are stories about three people who have gone far beyond the minimum standards in life.
These people not only did right but they also did it with the right attitude. They are my heroes and they have inspired me to be better.
I hope they will also inspire you.

Deb Says "Hey!"

"You know you're going bald if hand cream cures dandruff, the sun seems to be hotter, or you have the same bottle of shampoo after two years." I told those and other bald jokes to my bald friend, Debbie. Deb was bald because her head had been shaved for the surgery to remove a brain tumor, and the cancer therapy that followed had kept her bald. Deb's husband had told me that she didn't like the fact that her visitors were all treating her so cautiously because of her condition, so I figured I would liven things up a bit by confronting the obvious.

Deb was an "ordinary" housewife with two small boys, but she was anything but ordinary. Besides the usual descriptions — beautiful, smart, nice — she was, without question, the most impressive person I had ever met. The cancer that changed her world and finally took her life couldn't change her. For Deb, life was not about herself, but about relationships. When it became clear that her body was going to lose the battle with cancer, instead of being bitter she said, "I didn't ask 'why' when God gave me my loving husband and two wonderful boys and I'm not going to ask 'why' now that I'm dying of cancer. I'm just going to ask 'Who'?" For Deb, "who" was her "precious Jesus."

We all think being strong is about being tough. With Deb, weakness seemed to make her and those around her stronger. Before her first surgery, word got out that Deb was in the hospital. There was no organized effort to arrange anything special, but somehow a thousand hearts she had touched were drawn to circle the hospital creating an unbreakable human chain that was made up of nothing but weak links. Looking up at the third floor window my wife, three daughters, and I could see Deb, so weak she couldn't stand without leaning on her husband, but somehow so strong that we were encouraged in the midst of our discouragement. But that was Deb, she could always raise your spirits; even in her dying she made life more worth living. With tears streaming down my face I looked at my girls and told them, "This is one of the greatest things you will ever see in your lifetime. Remember it."

It's been about sixteen years and I still remember that night and the many difficult but amazing days and nights that followed for the next six months. I remember how she would say, "Hey!" in her beautiful southern accent. With that one word she would tell you that you were special to her and to God and that, no matter how bad things seemed, everything was going to be all right. Even when she was too weak to speak, she always said, "Hey!"

There were some days Deb only had a couple of hours of lucidity, but she would use those hours to comfort the nurses who were attending to her. When she wasn't lucid, nurses would stand by her door just to be close to her. Her one fear in dying was that her youngest son wouldn't remember her. Her hope was that she would live to his second birthday and that he would remember that day. She never made it and, near the end, when her husband suggested that she tape messages for her boys, she overcame her last fear. She told her husband that someday he would remarry and he would have a new wife and the boys would have a new mother. She told him that she would not make a tape because, "I refuse to be a ghost from the past that will get in the way of their relationship with their new mother."

Deb was the greatest person I ever met because, in this uncertain world with so many things to be afraid of, she knew that love was the opposite of fear. Life was simple for her: love God and love people — no more, no less. So when you're afraid, remember Deb says, "Hey!"

The Most Successful Man in the World

You know at funerals where your emotions are so raw and your memories are so vivid that you cry while you are laughing and laugh while you are crying? That's how I was at Clark's funeral. Clark was an ordinary guy, who lived an ordinary life, but somehow had an *extra*ordinary impact on those who knew him.

Clark was my best friend. If opposites attract in marriage, then that must also be the case for best friends. I was the skinny, studious type who was still playing with trucks while the rest of my friends were playing with girls. Clark, on the other hand, was a barrel-chested brawler who literally lived on the wrong side of the tracks. His parents had nothing but shared everything. They raised five boys and three girls in a one bedroom house that actually belonged to an uncle. Mom and Dad slept on a rollout couch, the girls in the bedroom, the five boys on one bed on the front porch, and the uncle in another bed on the porch. It was a horrible house but a great home.

After high school, I went to college and Clark went into the Navy. I ran track at school and he boxed for his ship. He had a crew cut and I had a ponytail. He fought in Vietnam and I protested the war. He went his way and I went mine.

Years later we ended up in the same town with our families. He had two boys and I had three girls. I was a financial advisor and he was a contractor. He was the extrovert who knew everyone and I was the introvert who knew no one. He was "hang loose" and I was uptight. I ate oatmeal for breakfast and he ate donuts. I played golf and he went fishing. I saw my children marry and I held my grandchildren. Clark never did.

Clark died of a heart attack at the age of 52. His wife got the call on her cell phone while driving. Being a nurse she knew what it meant when the conversation started, "Pull over and stop the car." It was not a small church, but it was packed to overflowing with people standing in the foyer and even outside. Looking around that sanctuary, you knew why Clark had such a big chest; he needed it to make room for his huge heart. His heart touched the young and the old, the rich and the poor, the successful and the failures. He touched people so deeply because he never held back; he gave everything he had, and then kept on giving. The priest said, "I didn't know this man, but he must have been a great man."

Shortly before he died, Clark built a family room addition onto our house. While he was doing it, he filled an old tire with cement as a base for my youngest daughter's tetherball pole. He scratched into the cement "To my friend Hillary, Clark." The kids haven't played tetherball in years. The ball and rope have rotted away, but the base and pole still stand in the middle of the yard as a tribute to my best friend. This past summer, Hillary got married. Before the wedding, I planted a bougainvillea next to that old tetherball pole and the vine climbed up it. Clark wasn't at the wedding but those flowers and his memory were.

The local American Legion baseball team has named their annual inspirational player award after Clark. The high school named the football field's press box in his honor.

Those are honors that will fade and people will forget who he was; it's a fate we all share. But Proverbs says, "The righteous man lives a blameless life, blessed are his children after him."[44] Clark loved his boys and that blessing will never fade. In his eulogy to his Dad his youngest son said, "Dad always felt like he was a failure because he never had much money, but I think he was the most successful man in the world."

The Most Generous Man I Know

Winston Churchill once said, "We make a living by what we get, but we make a life by what we give." I have a brother-in-law who has done both very well; the first by accident and the second on purpose.

If first impressions are hard to change, then it's amazing my family loves Jim because he made some horrible first impressions. My Dad couldn't get over a guy who tended bar at night and played golf all day. Mom was more opened-minded, but Jim did his best to change that. Mom flew to L.A. to meet Jim. He was supposed to pick her up at the airport, but he was a no-show. After picking up Mom, my sister headed to her apartment, worried about what had happened to Jim. The mystery was solved but the problem wasn't when she got his "one" phone call — asking her to come bail him out of jail. It seems he had set a record for unpaid parking tickets.

My first encounter with Jim wasn't so positive either, but that was hardly his fault. My sister was behind him screaming "hit him" at the top of her lungs while he attacked me with a vase. I had hitchhiked down to L.A. to meet my prospective brother-in-law and I got to my sister's apartment a few hours late. They had fallen asleep in front of the TV and the front door was too far from the living room for them to hear my pounding, so I went around to the back door to see if it was open. Prowling around her back door at two in the morning, they made the obvious assumption that I was a burglar. Thankfully, Jim didn't hit me and, thankfully, my sister married him, despite the misgivings of her family.

Jim is one of the most impressive people I have ever met — not for his accomplishments, which are incredible — but for his character. He was all *everything* in high school sports in New York City and an outstanding baseball player at Bucknell College. Gary Carter, the retired New York Mets catcher, told me Jim could have made it to the majors in baseball, and basketball was his best sport. On the PGA Champions Tour, he has won six times and he was one of the top money earners for a number of years, much to the surprise and delight of my father. But I have never once heard him brag about his accomplishments. Heck, if I were *half* the athlete he is, I would have Superman's "S" tattooed on my chest.

But what really makes Jim so impressive is his generosity. Generosity is hard to do because you literally have to put your money where your mouth is. In order to give to someone else, you have to give up something for yourself. It requires that you give up a little bit of your security, your needs, and your desires in order to affirm someone else. I enjoyed being the recipient of his generosity but I never really thought much about it until one day at a golf tournament in L.A., when I had a chance meeting with one of Jim's old college buddies. The old friend, who described himself as the "rich kid," said that everyone but Jim mooched off of him when they went out to the movies or for some tacos. I think he said something like, "Jim picked up the tab even when it took all he had." However, he made another comment that I'll always remember. He almost whispered, "I've been married three times and have four kids, and I don't know if any of them ever really liked me; but I know one person in the world likes me for *me* and not my money."

That's when it hit me. Generosity isn't so much about money as it is about demonstrating to someone else that you think they are more important than yourself. There used to be an ad that said, "I want to be like Mike" (Michael Jordan)[45], but I want to be like Jim, because the world's greatest athlete is no match for the most generous man I know.

You Can't Lose What You Give Away

"You've done it, you've reached financial security." Twenty-five years ago, as a young financial advisor, I heard that tag line for a television commercial and I actually audibly responded to the TV, "That's a lie; there is no such thing as financial security."

It would be nice if we lived in a world of certainty but we live in a world of chance. A smoker lives a long life and a jogger dies young, the best relay team drops the baton, a presidential election is decided by 327 disputed votes, and on 9/11 a person is at the wrong place at the wrong time. Chance can destroy a great plan and reward a sloppy one.

You can avoid many financial disasters but, because of chance, you can't eliminate them all. The unforeseen and the unknown are always lurking in the shadows. I was sharing a story the other day with a good friend about a school principal who was afraid that Y2K was going to cause a total financial collapse. So he sold everything and moved into a cabin in the woods where he could be self-sufficient. Y2K turned out to be a non-issue, but his attempt to avoid a perceived disaster resulted in a real disaster when his propane tank exploded, killing him. My friend related her own story about a co-speaker at a conference who was afraid to fly, so he arranged to have his speech video-conferenced from his office in the Twin Towers, on September 11, 2001 — where he died.

Financial security may be impossible, but financial peace of mind isn't. Financial peace of mind requires doing the things that can reduce financial risks (saving, limiting debt, and diversifying investments) and accepting the fact that they may not work. It also requires a generous attitude. It doesn't take a genius to realize that you can do two things with money, save it or spend it. Too much saving is hoarding and too much spending is self-indulgence. By limiting what you save for yourself and spend on yourself, you have money left over to be generous. And, in an odd way, this selflessness may be the most important part of financial peace of mind, and even financial security.

A finance professor at the local university used to have me talk to his graduating seniors. My speech was different from the usual, "This is how you get rich with a finance degree" speech. I would ask them who they thought was the most financially secure person in the world. Back then, the two most common answers were Donald Trump and the Shah of Iran. I replied by offering the name of Mother Theresa. If she got sick, there would be a plane waiting to take her to any hospital in the world. She could eat in any restaurant and sleep in any hotel and no one would dare charge her. Trump and the Shah could lose what they had (the Shah did) but Mother Theresa couldn't lose the goodwill she had accumulated.

Financial markets are scary right now, but don't lose hope. As my grandfather (who saw his private bank through the Great Depression) used to remind me, "Hard times mean good times are coming." So there is always hope, but even more important than hope is the peace of mind that comes from knowing that you can't lose what you give away.

Section 8

It's Up to You: Summary

"Integrity without knowledge is weak and useless, and knowledge without integrity is dangerous and dreadful."
- Samuel Johnson

This book has outlined your duties as a fiduciary and this section summarizes what you have learned. It is now your responsibility to apply what you know. How well you do that will depend on how diligently you carry out your duties and that is a function of not only your knowledge but also your integrity. So, do the right things and finish well.

Finishing Well

"You need to finish well." Those were words of warning and encouragement from a friend about how I should live my life. My college track coach used to say something similar, "You need to finish strong." To finish well in life, as well as in a race, you need to start well, hold that momentum as you progress, and finish without letting up.

This book has shown that, as a fiduciary, you have similar requirements. You start well by gathering information about your trust, pension, or charitable beneficiary's needs and the requirements of the law and controlling documents. You continue well by organizing the information, formulating a plan, and then implementing that plan. You finish well by routinely monitoring the needs of the beneficiary, the performance of the plans, and the circumstances of the environment. These steps constitute a prudent process as described in the Uniform Prudent Investor Act which "... imposes the obligation of prudence in the conduct of investment functions and... specifies the attributes of prudent conduct."

The Act and, hopefully, this book, make it clear that this standard of prudence is an "...objective [standard] rather than subjective...," which is the exact opposite of the quip by Supreme Court Justice Potter Stewart when, in frustration, he said he couldn't define pornography, "But I know it when I see it..." As a fiduciary, you are not held to some arbitrary standard of prudence which can be affected by whims or outcomes, but to a standard based on well-defined attributes of conduct which include the:

- Duty to consider the risk/return tradeoff
- Duty to exercise reasonable care
- Duty to exercise reasonable skill
- Duty to exercise reasonable caution
- Duty to evaluate investments in context of the whole portfolio (Portfolio Standard)
- Duty to consider risk tolerance
- Duty to consider time horizon
- Duty to monitor
- Duty to investigate
- Abrogating of categoric restrictions (no longer a list of approved investments)
- Duty of professional fiduciaries to exercise greater skill
- Duty to diversify
- Duty to consider investment correlations
- Duty to avoid uncompensated risk
- Duty to consider special circumstances
- Duties at inception
- Duty of loyalty
- Duty of impartiality
- Duty to incur costs that are appropriate and reasonable
- Duty to consider tax consequences
- Acknowledgement that fiduciary actions are not judged in hindsight
- Duty to consider delegation

Since uncertainty is a certainty, you can't always be right — so you must be prudent. Prudence is a process with duties defined in the Uniform Prudent Investor Act as listed above. As a fiduciary, these duties are the standards by which your actions are judged. I hope this book has encouraged you to be a better fiduciary and, in the words of my friend, I hope it has inspired you to finish well.

Endnotes

[1] *Jordan's 10 Greatest Commercials Ever*, ESPN.com Sports Business, February 17, 2009, Darren Rovell.
[2] *Friends*, 1994-2004, Bright/Kauffman/Crane Productions, Warner Bros. Television, National Broadcasting Company (NBC).
[3] *Cheers*, 1982-1993, Charles/Burrows/Charles Productions, Paramount Television, National Broadcasting Company (NBC).
[4] Modern Investment Management and the Prudent Man Rule, Bevis Longstreth (New York, NY: Oxford University Press, 1986), page 7.
[5] *The Birds*, 1963, Alfred J. Hitchcock Productions, Universal Pictures.
[6] *Black's Law Dictionary*, Sixth Edition by Henry Campbell Black (West Publishing Company, 1999), p. 1513
[7] *The Jerk*, 1979, Aspen Film Society, Universal Pictures.
[8] *Survivor*, 2000-..., Mark Burnett Productions, Castaway Television Productions, Columbia Broadcasting System (CBS).
[9] *Extreme Makeover: Home Edition*, 2003-..., American Broadcasting Company (ABC).
[10] *Welcome to My Nightmare*, Alice Cooper solo album, 1975, Atlantic (US) Anchor/ABC (UK); music concert film, 1976 (Dabill Productions).

[11] Canon Rebel EOS commercials, Andre Agassi, 1990-1991.
[12] *Statemaster* website: http://www.statemaster.com/encyclopedia/Knowledge-economy.
[13] *Brainy quote* website: http://www.brainyquote.com/quotes/authors/a/alexis_de_tocqueville.html.
[14] Taxpayer Beware: Bank Bailout Will Hurt, by Adam Davidson and Alex Blumberg, *Morning Edition*, February 27, 2009, http://www.npr.org/templates/story/story.php?storyId=101224460
[15] II Kings 20:16-21.
[16] The Greatest Generation, by Tom Brokaw (Random House, Inc., New York.)
[17] *The Official Arlo Guthrie* website: http://www.arlo.net/resources/lyrics/alices.shtml.
[18] http://www.Dictionary.com.
[19] *The Creature from the Black Lagoon*, 1954, Universal Pictures.
[20] *The Wizard of Oz*, 1939, Metro-Goldwyn-Mayer Studios (MGM).
[21] *The Naked City*, 1948, Hellinger Productions.
[22] *WKRP in Cincinnati*, 1978-1981, Company Four Production Company, Columbia Broadcasting System (CBS).
[23] *Doonesbury*, by Garry Trudeau, Universal Press Syndicate.
[24] *Paul Revere's Ride*, line 129, Henry Wadsworth Longfellow, 1860.
[25] Ibid., Line 127.
[26] *Casey at the Bat*, Ernest Lawrence Thayer, 1888.
[27] *Umpire's Code of Ethics* website: http://www.umpiring.qld.softball.org.au.
[28] *eHow* website: http://www.ehow.com/how_2079989_become-mlb-official.html.
[29] *Baseball Almanac* website: http://www.baseball-almanac.com/ws11/gam_ws.shtml.

[30] Paraphrase of quote by Jim McKay as host for ABC network's *Wide World of Sports*.
[31] The Uniform Prudent Investor Act, Official Comment, Article 1.1 Uniform Prudent Investor Act Prefatory Note.
[32] Uniform Prudent Management of Institutional Funds Act, Prefatory Note: Reasons for Revision.
[33] UPIA, Section 2, Comment: Abrogating categoric restrictions.
[34] *Restatement (Third) of Trusts (Prudent Investor Rule)* § 227, Comment f, page 25.
[35] "Confessions of a Fund Pro", *Money*, February 1999, pp. 73-75, Ted Aronson.
[36] "Is There Life After Babe Ruth?", *Barron's*, April 2, 1990.
[37] *Index Mutual Funds: Profiting from an Investment Revolution*, by W. Scott Simon, (Cataloging-in-Publication, 1998), page 103.
[38] Morningstar, Advanced Analytics, Legg Mason Value C, Analysis by Bridget B. Hughes, 11-25-08.
[39] "The Prescient Are Few", *The New York Times*, July 13, 2008, Mark Hilbert.
[40] Ibid., internal quote by Professor Russ Wermers.
[41] http://www.Dictionary.com
[42] News from Simon & Schuster: Book Review *Your Money & Your Brains: How the New Science of Neuroeconomics Can Help Make You Rich*, by Jason Zweig (Simon & Schuster, 2007)
[43] *The Cycle of Market Emotions*, Westcore Funds / Denver Investment Advisors LLC, 1998.
[44] Proverbs 20:7.
[45] 1992 Gatorade® commercial.

Ask Us About Prudent Investing, The Process for Handling Uncertainty!

Visit our financial advising website at:
http://www.elyportfolios.com

ELY PRUDENT PORTFOLIOS, LLC
Because You Can't Always be Right...
YOU MUST BE PRUDENT

We offer services to fiduciaries, professionals, and the general public.

<u>Consulting Services</u>

- **Fiduciary Analysis:** What fiduciaries don't know can expose them to personal liability and their portfolios to unnecessary risks, excess costs, and avoidable conflicts.
- **IRA Distributions:** Avoiding and correcting required minimum distribution problems.
- **Build a Prudent Portfolio:** Avoid "revenue sharing" and years of other unnecessary and hidden charges. Pay a one-time consulting fee to set up a low-cost index portfolio and pay for ongoing help only as needed.

<u>Investment Management</u>

Ely Prudent Portfolios manages selected portfolios on a limited basis, using low-cost, institutional, asset class funds provided by Dimensional (DFA). As a registered investment advisor, the firm is a fiduciary to all its management clients and accepts the delegation of investment and management functions by other fiduciaries. We specialize in managing portfolios for:

- Private Trusts
- Charitable Organizations
- IRA Rollovers

<u>To Book Guerdon Ely as a Guest Speaker</u>

Call 1-800-560-0636 or
http://www.elyportfolios.com/contactus

CPSIA information can be obtained at www.ICGtesting.com
Printed in the USA
BVOW001642160513

320914BV00001B/1/P